Walking th
Cornish Folklore

Margaret Caine & Alan Gorton

A Comfy Jack Book

First published in 2005 by Cotswold Quality (Leisure) Ltd.
4, Gables Court, Blackwell, Warwickshire CV36 4PE

ISBN 0 9541036 3 7

Cover designed by NPD Design Consultants, Shipston-on-Stour CV36 4AH
Printed and bound by R Booth Ltd
Antron Hill, Mabe, Penryn, Cornwall TR10 9HH

Contents

Introduction

This book has wide appeal. It is essential reading for anyone interested in folklore, in walking, and in combining the two. By vividly bringing to life the legendary heroes, alluring mermaids, terrifying giants, mischievous piskeys and infamous wreckers together with exhilarating walks specially designed to give you the excitement of seeking out their locations, stepping over the very ground they trod, it doubles the pleasure. You will visit remarkable places which might be atmospheric, peaceful, brooding or offer a magnificently high, windy viewpoint, dramatic cliffs, crescent-shaped sandy beaches, sheltered creeks of lazy rivers and stark moors ancient and unspoiled. This is the essence of where you will walk. But there is more. The addition of imaginative stories adds a new dimension - a journey through both a real and a mythical landscape.

Not for nothing is Cornwall known as the 'Land of Legend'. Its folklore reaches to the mists of time with such a rich diversity, such a distinctive heritage, that scarcely a hamlet is without its own story. In this fascinating patchwork people live on the edge of two worlds, the material and the mysterious, where fact and fiction overlap - so here are real people, historical figures whose lives have been embroidered with help from the supernatural, sunken cities, village wenches turned into stone, all within a realm of fairies, spriggans and knockers, those curious creatures of the netherworld - reminders of a past so culturally different, more physically demanding and dangerous than our own times. This book illuminates this Cornish past and will enhance your interest in the county.

Here though is more than just a collection of the great and lesser known Cornish myths and legends. Necessarily we have been selective in choosing from the hundreds still surviving those which have caught our imagination or the versions we like best. Where there is a historical basis, we have consulted contemporary records. At the same time we have aimed to show how fine the county is on foot. To enable you to identify locations, map references are given using OS Landranger series. The maps accompanying each walk are intended for guidance only, and are not to scale. We would ask you, though, to park carefully and considerately in small villages and lanes and at all times to follow the Countryside Code.

Using this book, your journey will be one of exploration of the quality that makes Cornwall a place apart. We hope it will inspire you to follow in our footsteps and experience the thrill of discovery for yourselves. It has not been possible to do justice to the whole county in one volume, so this one has a companion, *Footloose in Cornwall's Folkore*, which covers the rest of the county.

Now we shall a tale unfold ...

Margaret Caine and Alan Gorton

MORWENSTOW

CRUEL COPPINGER, WRECKER AND PLUNDERER ...

On the remote northern tip of Cornwall a winter's storm rages along the coast. A ship, its sails in tatters, is driven before the howling wind into the boiling seas of Harty Race, as it struggles to avoid the treacherous rocks. Old sailors gave it a chilling reputation:

From Padstow Point to Lundy Light
Is a watery grave, by day or night.

Most people have battened their doors and shuttered their windows against the lashing rain. Not all. An anxious, excited throng has gathered on the shore, eagerly watching the drama unfold. Around here a heavily-laden foreign ship thrown on the rocks is a blessing - it brings food, clothes, timber, sailcloth, ropes, equipment, perhaps even jewels and gold.

Rolling in the trough of the sea the ship foundered and broke into pieces. One by one the crew perished, swept off the pitching decks to be drowned in the towering waves or battered to death on the razor-sharp rocks. All except one. In full view of the watchers a tall, broad figure plunged overboard and with powerful strokes battled his way through the seething surf. He struggled onto the beach, emerging from the waves spitting, brushing his hair from his eyes, and despite his exhaustion, vaulted onto a horse, grasped the bridle and shouting in some foreign tongue forced the young female rider to take him to her house. Spurred on by the stranger the animal galloped straight to the farm where the girl, Dinah Hamlyn, lived with her parents. Here he was treated as any survivor of shipwreck, given food and dry clothes - but then refused to leave. He began to dress himself in his host's best clothes. He took his place at the family table and on the settle by the hearth. Despite this unpromising beginning, within a few weeks the stranger had been given a job on the farm.

There was though something different about him. He rarely talked of himself and never, ever mentioned his past. The Hamlyns discovered only that he was Danish and named David Coppinger - nothing more. Nonetheless he laboured doggedly on the land with the strength of five men and for this reason alone they were pleased he had descended on them so inexplicably. The other workers took a different view. They encountered the violent, unpredictable temper which he hid from the Hamlyns, and gossiped about how attentive he was to the unsophisticated Dinah.

In less than a year Farmer Hamlyn died and after an unseemly short interval which set local tongues wagging, Coppinger married Dinah and gained ownership of the farm and stock. At first all seemed well, but as the joy of married bliss wore off Coppinger revealed himself to be a brutal, sadistic husband and employer. Though he had taken over the control and management of the farm, the widowed Mrs Hamlyn, Dinah's mother, had been left with a considerable amount of money. He soon began to get this by instalments of force, tying his wife to her bedstead and threatening to flog her with a whip unless Mrs Hamlyn transferred to him what he wanted. In almost no time at all he had got his hands on it all. Now he began to lose interest in the farm. It quickly deteriorated as he turned back to the sea for his livelihood, not as a sailor or fisherman like the other local men, but as the savage leader of a fearsome gang of wreckers and smugglers. It became a rendezvous and refuge for every unsavoury character along this coast.

It didn't take Coppinger long to establish a reign of terror which would last for years. First, he set up a smuggling network and unknown ships began to appear more and more frequently on the coast as signals flashed from the headlands to lead them to the safest creek or cove. Then his gang were organised into actually wrecking ships, luring them onto the rocks below the cliffs where Coppinger lived, before plundering their cargo: threatened by their leader's violence, they showed no mercy to shipwrecked sailors or to Excisemen who had the misfortune to catch them at work. The Revenue men learned to keep their distance after one of their number had his head chopped off by the gang on the gunwale of his boat. Reluctant locals were 'persuaded' by threats of violence to join the gang. Gentry and clergy were cowed into submission. Coppinger acquired a full-rigged schooner, *The Black Prince*, to enhance his unlawful activities. On one occasion, skippered by Coppinger himself, she led a pursuing Revenue cutter into an intricate channel near Gull Rock from where, thanks to his knowledge of the bearings, *The Black Prince* escaped unscathed while the King's vessel foundered and all on board were drowned.

As he continued, Coppinger exercised exclusive control over a network of bridle-paths along the fields, issuing orders that no man was to pass over 'Coppinger's Tracks' at night - and no-one did unless on his business. He piled his booty, kegs of brandy, chests of tea and iron-strapped boxes containing money and jewels, in 'Coppinger's Cave' within the towering 300-foot cliff at Steeple Brink, which could only be reached by rope-ladder.

Eventually, the forces of the law and the Revenue banded together in a concerted effort to capture Coppinger and his gang. In a pre-planned ambush the majority were killed. Coppinger himself escaped but the Revenue men maintained such vigilance, stationing armed King's cutters just off-shore, day and night, that the county became too hot for him. One night, during a howling storm similar to the one which had announced his arrival, an unidentified ship hove-to off Harty Pool. A rocket hissed from Gull Rock and a gun from the ship answered the signal. A boat was lowered, fighting its way to shore where Coppinger waited, brandishing a cutlass and cursing. As soon as he was aboard the ship it spread canvas and sailed into the teeth of the storm. Cruel Coppinger was never to return.

If this is the folk-tale, what do we know of Cruel Coppinger in reality? He appears to be semi-fictional. On 23 December 1792 the only survivor of a shipwreck was washed ashore amongst the surf and rocks near Welcombe Mouth. A local yeoman farmer of Golden Park near Hartland, William Arthur, gave him shelter. Within a year of this unexpected arrival, the parish register of Hartland for 1793 records that "*Daniel Herbert Coppinger of the King's Royal Navy and Ann Hamlyn mard (by licence) 3 Aug*." There is though no record of a Coppinger among the commissioned officers of the Navy. The bride was not the daughter of his host, but the forty-two-year-old eldest daughter of Ackland and Ann Hamlyn of Galsham, Devon. When Ann's mother died in 1800, Ann and her husband succeeded to the property. He must have spent his fortune quickly for in 1802 he was registered as bankrupt and then a prisoner before the King's Bench; with him was a Richard Copinger, a merchant from Martinique. From then, nothing more is known about what happened to him - perhaps he was indeed spirited away in a mysterious ship - but Ann Hamlyn died, aged 82, at Barnstaple on 31 August 1833 and was buried next to her mother in Hartland church. These few hints about Coppinger became the foundation of a myth.

... AND A NYMPH WHO LEFT US HER NAME

Tamara was a beautiful nymph. Her parents were earth spirits and she was born in a cavern deep underground near Morwenstow. From an early age though she loved the day-light. Whenever possible she escaped from the cavern, revelling in the warmth of the sun, thrilling to the songs of birds and when she was older swimming in the clear, chattering streams - all the activities that her parents shunned. Though young, she was no more wilful than other nymphs but her parents were concerned about her, warning her of the consequences of visiting the upper world without their knowledge. They had good reason: they wished to protect her from the Giants of the moors whose unwelcome attentions they had experienced.

As she grew up Tamara - young, heedless - took every opportunity to be in the sunshine. It was on one of these occasions that two sons of Dartmoor giants - Tavy and Tawrage - saw her. She was indeed very beautiful, even by earth-nymph standards, and she captured the hearts of both. How they tried and tried to attract her! But in response to their efforts Tamara led them a merry chase over the moorlands, teasing and tantalising them.

One day Tavy and Tawrage saw Tamara under a bush in Morwenstow, and agreed that the time had come when she really must decide which of them she preferred and would marry.

They called her by every endearing name that Giants know. They pleaded. They used every argument they could think of. Meanwhile her parents had missed Tamara, and began to look for her - and were angry when they found her and especially the company she was in, seated between these sons of Giants whom they hated. First, Tamara's father cast a spell which made both Tavy and Tawrage fall asleep. Then he tried to persuade his daughter to return to their underground home. Tamara refused. Becoming even more angry at what he saw as wilful stubbornness the father cursed his daughter, so strongly that Tamara dissolved in tears. So great were these that they quickly became a pure, crystal stream, first bubbling from a marshy meadow then gliding southwards from Morwenstow towards the sea. By the curse Tamara had been transformed into a river of tears which would flow forever into the ocean.

After some time Tavy awoke. His Tamara had gone and he ran to his father on the moor. The Giant, omniscient as some giants are, was aware of her metamorphosis and to ease his son's anguish transformed him into a stream, too. Rushing over rocks, running through clefts, sliding through valleys, to this day Tavy searches for Tamara, meandering hither and thither, calling to his love - and remains content running alongside her until their waters merge in their journey to the sea.

Tawrage took longer to wake up, but as soon as he did he knew what had happened. He ran into the hills seeking magical help so that he too might be changed into a stream. He had made a fundamental mistake though: he mistook the route his adored Tamara had taken. Now, ever sorrowing, he flows in the opposite direction away from his beloved.

And we remember them every time we cross the Tamar, the Tavy and the Taw.

WALK DIRECTIONS

Distance	7½ miles (11.7km)	Time	3½ hours
Map	OS Landranger 190 205155	Terrain	There are well-defined but steep inland paths at the beginning and the Coast Path has steep parts, from 30 feet (10m) to 475 feet (144m), some of which are strenuous.

Car Parking: Park opposite Morwenstow church

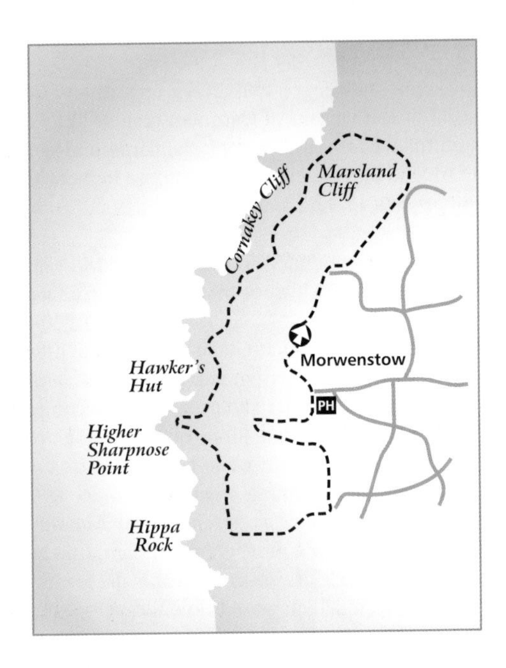

\>> Go through the lychgate at Morwenstow church and turn right, taking the gravel path downhill through the churchyard.
There can be few churches with a more dramatic location, on the edge of a small valley which within half a mile tumbles to the sea. For forty years from 1834 until his death in 1875 the eccentric clergyman Robert Stephen Hawker was vicar here, deeply concerned that all shipwrecked sailors and passengers were given a Christian burial. The churchyard contains several of their graves. The figurehead of the 'Caledonia', wrecked in 1842, is on your left, a stark and poignant reminder of the perils of this coastline. By the 'Upper Trees' a tall granite cross bearing the words 'Unknown Yet Well Known' marks the site of a communal grave of many victims of the sea on this remote northern tip.

\>> Climb the stone stile at the bottom of the churchyard and turn left, skirting to the right of the Old Vicarage, and into a small copse.
You will be interested by the chimneys on the Old Vicarage. These were designed by 'Parson' Hawker as miniatures of and representing church towers where he had served prior to his appointment here. The fifth chimney is a model of his mother's tomb.

>> Ignore the small path on your left but go along the side of the barn and down to the footbridge at the bottom of the valley. Cross this and follow the path as it rises steeply out from the trees, keeping to the right-hand boundary of the field. Keep straight on at a footpath junction and pass through a gate at the top of the field, still with the hedge on your right You continue to climb, through two fields to a ladder stile. At the next gate turn right and go between the buildings at Westcott Farm. After about 100 yards (90m) the track veers to the right, but you walk straight on, keeping to the right of the hedge to a stile. Continue to follow the waymark to Yeolmouth where you arrive at a lane, and in about 25 yards (22m) turn left to take the signed surfaced path around Cornakey Farm to a track into a field. Several fields away you can see Marsland Manor, where you are heading.

>> Continue along the top of the field following the hedge on our left for 50 yards (45m) before leaving the field at the gate in the left-hand boundary. Turn right onto a track, walking between tall hedges. Pass one field and cross diagonally left the next to a stone stile near the corner, then across the next field, still heading towards Marsland Manor, to another stile just before you enter woodland. Cross a stile and go down a steep bank by rough-cut steps, going over the footbridge and up again, along part of an ancient track between steep banks. At the top, where there is a footpath junction, bear right following the waymark, walking towards a row of trees. Immediately after the trees bear right and then left along the top edge of the field. Cross the stile onto the lane at the rear of Marsland Manor. Here you turn left and after a further 200 yards (185m), where the road bends to the right at the junction take the lane signed 'Unsuitable For Motors', turn left again onto a track signed 'Marsland Mouth' and the 'Coast Path'. Go through the gate and descend for about 200 yards (185m) to where the path divides: follow the yellow arrow to Marsland Mouth. At the next fork keep right, still on the descending track.

The stream in the valley below on your right is the boundary between Cornwall and Devon.

The track continues to descend to Marsland Mouth, but turn off uphill left onto the Coast Path.

>> You now climb steeply for quite some way, crossing a stile to arrive at a (welcome) seat at the top of Marsland Cliff, where you can regain your breath.

>> Continue on the Coast Path, descending into Litter Mouth by the steps and cross the footbridge before ascending steeply again up the other side, though this time there are no steps to help with a hard slog. Stay on the Coast Path, along Cornakey Cliff.

On your left is the contorted strata of Gull Rock, from where Cruel Coppinger left Cornwall on that dark, stormy night.

>> Continue on the Coast Path, crossing a total of five stiles before descending into Yeol Mouth. Cross another footbridge and climb up the other side. Follow the Coast Path waymarks along Henna Cliff, a short stretch of level ground before yet another up and down, descending from Henna Cliff, crossing the stream by the footbridge and taking the stepped path up to Vicarage Cliff.

It is worthwhile stopping here for a moment and taking in the views. "A stretch of bold rocky shore, an interchange of lofty headland and deep and sudden gorge, the valleys rushing with torrents which bound rejoicingly to the sea." How right 'Parson' Hawker was!

>> Continue along the Coast Path until you see a sign on your right to 'Hawker's Hut'.
It is worth taking this short diversion. The hut is made of driftwood dragged from the rocks below and here 'Parson' Hawker wrote his correspondence and poems, contemplated and smoked opium, while watching for ships in distress.

>> Return to the Coast Path, negotiate the wooden stile and head towards the whale-back shaped headland of Higher Sharpnose Point.
It was on the rocks below that the 'Caledonia' foundered in 1842 with the loss of all hands. If you walk to the edge to see for yourself just what peril faced the crew, take extreme care: it is more dangerous than it appears!

>> You now have a steep descent to the Tidna Shute Valley, one of those steep-sided combes on this coast where little streams have cut sheer-sided valleys to reach the sea. Cross the Tidna stream and go over two stiles before the breath-catching climb to an old Coastguard Station. All along this section the convolutions of the rock strata are particularly interesting. Now you pass through them to the stile to where the Coast Path diversion takes you away from the edge, as the rockface is eroding, and up a narrow valley for a short distance to a stile and two wooden walkways.

>> Follow the broad path alongside the fence of the field, crossing a stile and keeping to the edge of the field until you cross a further wooden walkway to the path which leads left between the wire fence and a hedge. Ignore the waymark which points straight ahead, but turn left along the path which climbs gradually inland. Cross a stile onto a broader track, then further stiles until you reach a gate leading to a lane. Follow this lane to your left until you reach a stone stile on your left opposite Stanbury Farm.

>> Head across the field to a stile, and across this second field to a wooden stile. Go past Tonacombe to a wooden stile opposite a tall metal gate. Now your track passes into a small copse which you leave by crossing two stiles into a small field. Leave this by a stile at the side of a gate and follow the right hand side of the next field descending to a stile that puts you onto a narrow track.

>> Continue to descend into the woods of the Tidna Valley, and cross a wooden stile to where there is a junction with other paths. At this point take the right fork, still descending to a stream which you can cross by a wooden walkway. Go past the National Trust sign and over a stile. Turn right up steps to reach a wooden stile. Continue to climb upwards across this field to reach a further stile.

>> Turn left and cross a stile. You can now see the Bush Inn at Morwenstow. Go towards the left hand side of the Inn, through a metal gate and emerge onto the road. Turn left and return to your car.

BOSCASTLE

A SILENT TOWER ...

Just before the serpentine coast road descends to Boscastle harbour, the old church of St Symphorian stands exposed on bare Forrabury Hill - and its squat tower from which an unusual legend stems.

This church has one marked contrast to its neighbour at Tintagel. Although there the bells rang out calling to the faithful, the tower at Forrabury stood silent for centuries: it had no bells. To make matters worse, Tintagel's bells have always been particularly harmonious and musical and when the wind blew towards Boscastle, seamen used the sound to guide them to the safety of the harbour. It was only after St Symphorian's church had been built that realisation dawned: this was not good enough, the bells the congregation could hear were not their own but their neighbours'. So they decided to buy "*as choice a peal as money could procure*", certainly to rival the chimes at Tintagel. An appeal was mounted, the Lord of the Manor, Lord de Bottreaux subscribed handsomely "*for the benefit of his soul, lords being in those good old days as careful of their souls as persons less loftily born*", and after a great deal of effort and fund raising an order was sent to a reputable London foundry. The bells were cast, blessed "*by the most exemplary dignity of the hierarchy*" and despatched by sea.

The weather was calm, the wind fair, the voyage went well and soon the ship was standing off Tintagel Head waiting for the evening tide to carry her into Boscastle harbour. Standing in the wheelhouse beside the steersman, the pilot listened for Tintagel vespers bells swinging along the waves. Kneeling, crossing himself, he reverently gave thanks to God for their safe voyage. The captain's retort was unequivocal: it had nothing to do with God but they should thank themselves, and especially himself, for skilled seamanship. "*Thank the ship, you fool. Thank God upon the shore.*" The pilot remonstrated, but the captain only laughed louder, "*You are a fool, I tell 'ee. Thank thyself and a steady helm*": all they needed now was the pilot's judgment for a safe landing. The argument continued. The pilot became more disturbed by the captain's blasphemy, while the captain grew angrier, jeering at the pilot's 'superstition' until his oaths rose above the roar of the wind and the waves. He wouldn't let the matter drop. The pilot could only remind him of God's retribution.

By now the ship was within sight of the church tower whose bells were soon to rival those of Tintagel. People thronged the cliffs at Willapark, watching anxiously the arrival of the precious freight for which they had worked so hard. But the captain was not to go unpunished. The watchers noticed the wind rising rapidly, blowing furiously from the west, whipping up the waves, driving the ship into the bay. Then they saw a monstrous wave rise far out to sea and roll inexorably landward. When less than half a mile from land, a mile from the church tower, the wave struck the vessel. She lurched to port and within an instant went down, bells and all. Fishermen rushed to the assistance of the stricken crew, but only the devout pilot was rescued - all the others were lost. As the ship sank, the new bells tolled with a muffled, mournful sound as if ringing her death-knell. The storm continued to rage and again the peal of bells was heard, dull and solemn but clearly distinguishable from the fury of the wind and the waves.

Even now you can hear them, just as when they were engulfed by the wild Atlantic. From its depths they warn of approaching winter storms that rage against this coastline. Reflect on the reason why!

... A TRUNCATED TOWER

Less than a mile away, another church has an interesting tower, though very different from that at Forrabury. St Merteriana's church at Minster stands on the steep slope of a valley. At first glance it looks as if the builders didn't complete their job, but left the tower with a saddleback roof instead of the usual battlements and pinnacles. Don't, though, be deceived by this: it is not what folklore tells us. There was a time when the tower was much taller in which the monks from the Priory here used to put a light to guide pilgrims on their dangerous route to the saint's shrine. Because of its location and its height this light was visible not only from inland but from the seaward end of the long, winding entrance to Boscastle harbour, constantly misleading the fishermen, sometimes with tragic consequences. After a particularly nasty accident, the fishermen were enraged. In a large group they walked up the valley and pulled down the tower, reducing it to its present height. It has never been rebuilt.

... AND WITCHES WHO SOLD THE WIND

Then there are the Boscastle witches. For centuries they were famous for gathering at the tortuous entrance to the harbour at sailing times and 'selling the wind'. A sailor who wanted a fair wind would buy a length of white string in which the witch would tie three knots, charging a coin for each. Undoing the first knot would bring a breeze to sail by, the second would keep a gale behind the ship, and the third was best for the wind that would guide him into the dangerous entrance to the harbour. Conversely, the witches could sell rope to bring on a storm - and raging storms which cause wrecks are blamed on a notorious local wrecker who persuaded a witch to 'sell him the wind'.

WALK DIRECTIONS

Distance	3½ miles	Time	1¾ hours
Map	OS Landranger 190 101914	Terrain	The first section is mainly gentle along a woodland valley, but later there is a steep climb on the road and on the Coast Path.

Car Park: Park in the central Boscastle car park, next to the North Cornwall Visitor Centre.

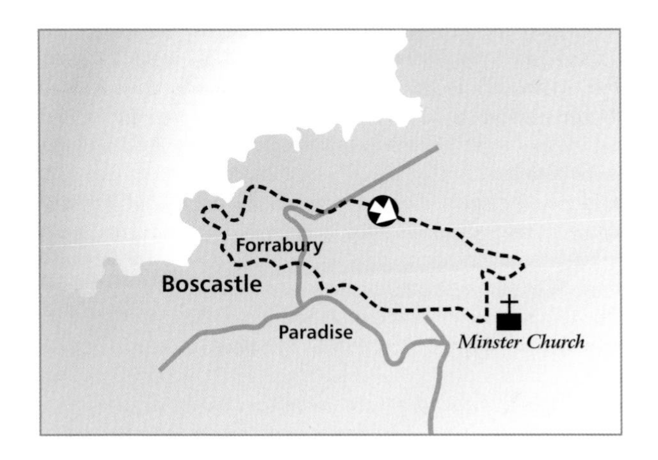

>> Go to the opposite end of the car park from the Visitor Centre to where a small wooden gate leads onto your path into the Valency Valley, famous for its associations with the novelist and poet Thomas Hardy, and central to his novel *A Pair of Blue Eyes*.

>> Follow the hedge on your left and go through the kissing gate. Continue up the valley, into the woodland, and through another kissing gate until you reach a large wooden bridge. Here a footpath sign indicates the route to Minster church on the opposite bank. Cross the stream and follow the path, ascending steeply up the side of the valley.

>> Follow the path as it meanders through Peter's Wood. At the waymark post and a junction in the path bear right. Go through the kissing gate to Minster church, surrounded by trees and eerily enclosed by the sides of the valley, as it was built in a natural amphitheatre which makes both a delightful and dramatic setting.
Robert Hawker's description captures the atmosphere:

> *"The Minster of the Trees! A lonely dell*
> *Deep with grey oaks, and 'mid their quiet shade*
> *Grey with the moss of years, yon antique cell."*

The magnificent views across the valley and down to the sea are a reward for your effort but illustrate just how easy it would be for the fishermen to be disoriented by a light in the church tower if it was any taller

There has been a religious settlement on this site since c. AD 500 when Madryn, a Welsh princess, settled to pray and to heal the sick. Her holy well lay to the north of the church but almost nothing remains of it. This part of the wood is haunted by monks from the twelfth-century Benedictine monastery which stood here until the fifteenth century, as they wander through the trees and the monastery's former gardens.

>> Follow the metalled path up to the right, until you reach a wooden gate leading onto a country lane. Turn right here, then right again when the lane forks. In a short distance the road curves to the left, but follow the footpath sign straight ahead, leading over a stone stile into a field. Cross this field, aiming towards the bottom left corner by the buildings. Go through the wooden gate between a cottage and a pond, turn right and cross the yard, then follow the signs up the track straight ahead, which runs between some more houses before you emerge onto a road.

>> Turn right and follow the road downhill, turning right along the street and past the Post Office. At the fork in the road take the left branch, cross over and continue up Forrabury Hill. Where the road curves to the right, follow the footpath sign to the coast, also on your right. Continue upwards through the trees and through a small gate onto the farmland.

Here you are on the edge of ancient grassland, Forrabury Common, which is still strip-farmed in Anglo-Saxon fashion. Long, narrow rectangles, bounded by low banks called 'stitches' are cultivated individually during Spring and Summer but thrown open to common grazing in the winter months.

>> Keep to the footpath which runs along the edge of the stitches and on the right of the hedge which borders the church of St Symphorian. A small gate leads into the churchyard.

You may wish to check that there are no bells in the tower - and find one inscribed JOHN TINK 1812. He lived at Welltown Manor, near Trevalga, and donated this one single bell sixty-two years after the tower was rebuilt on its original base.

>> Retrace your steps to the path along the edge of the stitches and head towards the sea. At a T-junction with the Coast Path turn right towards Willapark headland, with its white look-out building.

This was originally built in the 1820s as a 'pleasure house' by Thomas Avery, a successful merchant and some say a smuggler. Look across the fields to the churchtower: you can see the inspiration for Avery's design.

>> Return to the Coast Path and descend steeply into Boscastle harbour.

It is so shut in by steep black slopes of wild land and jagged rocks that it is difficult to believe that despite the vicious entrance the port was busy, bringing in coal and limestone to make fertiliser, as well as other goods from Bristol, and exporting slate from Delabole Quarry inland.

Walk parallel to the harbour, then take the steps down to the side opposite the Museum of Witchcraft.

It was here that the witches 'sold the wind', and in the macabre Museum is a witch with spikes driven through her skeleton when she was buried, to keep her down.

>> Turn right and walk past the telephone box. The car park from where we started is across the road.

TINTAGEL

KING ARTHUR: HISTORY, LEGEND OR FACT?

The legend of King Arthur is one of the most enduring and romantic. And it starts here.

When Uther Pendragon was arranging his coronation as King of England he summoned together his most powerful nobles. Amongst these was Gorlois, Duke of Cornwall, who took his young and beautiful wife Ygraine. This was the first time Uther had met Ygraine and the moment he set eyes on her after the ceremony he was smitten. He tried to seduce her but Ygraine was not impressed, resisted his advances and told her husband, asking to be taken back to Cornwall. Gorlois did just that and hid her away in his impregnable castle at Tintagel. However, expecting repercussions from Uther, Gorlois took his band of men to another stronghold nearby, Castle Dimilioc.

Despite Ygraine's absence, Uther's impulsive lust showed no signs of abating, and he turned for help to Merlin the wizard. Merlin came up with a cunning plan: he could transform Uther to resemble Duke Gorlois, for one night only, during which he could be with Ygraine. Uther grasped the scheme and marched to Cornwall where his army surrounded Gorlois, while he went on to Tintagel.

All this time Ygraine had been expecting her husband to return so showed no alarm when 'Gorlois' arrived at Tintagel. Nor did the guards challenge the transformed Uther as he approached and sought entry to the castle: he walked through its defences and straight to Ygraine's bedchamber. The future King Arthur was the consequence.

That was as far as Tintagel's association with King Arthur went, when it was first proposed by the Norman-Welsh cleric and peripatetic chronicler Geoffrey of Monmouth in his *Historia Regum Britanniae*, 'History of the Kings of Britain', published in 1136. His was the first major story - and a fanciful one at that - in which Arthur was a central figure but Geoffrey wrote only that Tintagel was where Arthur was conceived. Nowhere did he mention that this is where he was born or lived. Moreover the Arthur of Geoffrey was an aggressive war-lord, intent on creating an empire stretching to the walls of Rome itself. He was not the romantic, chivalric, honourable knight who spent his time jousting. These embellishments came later, introduced over the next three hundred years by other imaginative writers, until the whole corpus was collected and edited in about 1471 by Sir Thomas Malory and his *Morte d'Arthur*, the first storybook printed in English on Caxton's press, in 1485.

It is indeed a romatic tale. How can you possibly go wrong with a boy born to a mother whose first husband was slain by his usurper but who only found out early the next morning when she and Uther were awakened with news that during the night fighting had broken out at Dimilioc and that Gorlois had been defeated and killed. Horrified at what had happened between them, Ygraine demanded to know the true identity of the man she had thought was her husband. Only then did Uther reveal who he was. Nonetheless, despite this inauspicious start, Uther and Ygraine married soon afterwards. Just how willing she was we do not know but later she and Uther had a second child, a daughter Morgan le Fay. It was by her that Arthur had his own natural son, Mordred, not knowing that it was an incestuous relationship.

Before then Arthur had been brought up under the supervision of Merlin. When explaining his plan to Uther, Merlin had set one condition: he should raise any child of the illicit union. As soon as Ygraine had given birth the tiny baby was wrapped in a cloth of gold, taken through secret passages under the castle and handed to Merlin in the cave in which he was living. Merlin took the infant Arthur and fostered him with Sir Hector and his family, ensuring child's safety by keeping his parentage a closely guarded secret. Only when Uther died did Merlin produce the child, who proved his claim to be king by drawing a sword from a block of stone, before acquiring another, the enchanted Excalibur, from the mysterious Lady of the Lake. Now King of England, Arthur married Guinevere and ruled from his palace of Camelot, with his chivalrous knights who had a Round Table so that none should feel more important by sitting near its head. At Camelot the only flaw is the betrayal of Arthur by the adulterous love between Sir Lancelot, hitherto the most chivalrous and bravest of Arthur's knights, and Queen Guinevere. Years later that love is to destroy the Round Table, Arthur and all his knights, as Arthur's son Mordred, the one he fathered with his half-sister, Morgan le Fay, uses it to foment rebellion and eventual battle with Arthur.

But are you really sure it is only a story? Was Arthur's castle really at Tintagel? Of all the hundreds of Arthurian locations in Britain, Tintagel is the only one which claims to have been his birthplace. Why did Geoffrey chose this site, as he himself was a stranger to it? Was it because even then the history of the place conformed to its natural features, equally wild and grand, a promontory jutting out into the Atlantic, almost insulated in a sea of mystery?

All that existed on this headland in Geoffrey of Monmouth's time were the jumbled remains of early buildings and a huge ditch on the approach to its narrow neck. The castle ruins we see today perched on the dark crags were not here - they are clearly medieval and to a certain extent a monument to Geoffrey's inventive imagination. Recent excavations have revealed evidence that from the fifth to the seventh century here was a stronghold, a place of considerable importance and possibly a seasonal or ceremonial seat of the Kings of Dumnonia, the tribe of Celts whose lands covered the whole of Cornwall and parts of Devon. Work on building this Norman castle began in 1141, five years after Geoffrey's *Historia* had been published, for Richard, a natural son of Henry I and brother of Henry II, who had been created Earl of Cornwall in 1127 - despite Geoffrey calling Gorlois 'Duke of Cornwall' there was no such title then, not until the first Dukedom was bestowed on the Black Prince by his father King Edward III in 1337. Here had been a seat of power so important to the Cornish, particularly that of King Mark who once ruled Cornwall and Brittany from this bleak headland, that the Earl considered it politic to build a castle - after Geoffrey had wedded it firmly to the Arthur legend. For the folklore though it doesn't matter that the castle was built some 700 years after Arthur was saving us from the Anglo-Saxons - it looks right.

Even today, no single name fires our imagination more than that of King Arthur. His magic is present and potent. That in itself presents an enigma. Look in the history books and you won't find any reference to him. Yet after 1,500 years the folk memory remains as strong as ever. So was there an Arthur at all - did such a man ever exist? If so, who was he? What did he actually do? Legends abound. Facts are few.

The question of whether he existed is not easily answered. There are no contemporary records and we must rely to a large extent on conjecture. After the Romans had withdrawn in 410 AD, people from Germany, Jutland and Fresia were invited into the country as mercenaries by

Celtic warlords. Once here, they saw easy pickings. Without Rome's armies and with many of the Celtic tribes fighting each other, boatloads of warriors began raiding the country. It is at this point that the story of Arthur really begins. What little evidence we possess mentions a charismatic leader of part-Roman, part-British blood who welded together the feuding Celtic tribes into a force strong enough to drive the Saxons back to the coast. We cannot say for sure that this leader was called Arthur; what we can be reasonably certain of is that such a person, born in the late fifth or sixth century, existed. Though he may have been born and died in Cornwall, it is most unlikely that he fought the Saxons here for in his day their frontier still lay a hundred miles beyond the Tamar.

So is any of the legend real, and if so, what? If the historical Arthur ever existed, he was certainly not the fairy-tale king we imagine. At best he was an obscure chieftain of the fifth or sixth century, and certainly not 'King of England'. He bore little resemblance to the fifteenth-century hero of Malory's *Morte d'Arthur* and none to the Victorian gentleman celebrated by Tennyson in his *Idylls of the King*, nor to Hollywood's version. We must discard any picture of medieval knights in shining armour, and replace it with that of an earlier era when armour was hardly worn and certainly did not shine: at best, a leather jacket was the only protection in battle.

Was he in Cornwall? Even a brief visit to those sites relatively close to Tintagel which are associated with him offers a diversity of landscapes to add to the tales of magic and adventure. There is one tradition that Castle-an-Dinas, the earthwork near St Columb, served as Arthur's lodge while hunting over the marshy wilds of Goss Moor. On one occasion his horse left a footprint in a rock which we can see on the capstone of the destroyed Devil's Quoit. Another says that Arthur had a fortress named Kelliwic or Celli Wig, which could well be Castle Canyke, sometimes called Kelly Rounds, near Bodmin, which even then commanded the important trans-peninsular route (now the A30). Then within the broad expanse of Bodmin Moor we find 'King Alfred's Hall', 'King Arthur's Downs' and 'King Arthur's Bed', a roughly man-shaped natural rock basin on Trewartha Tor, and 'Arthur's Oven', the Iron Age cromlech.

There are still some elements outstanding on our route through the folklore. A major activity of Arthur's knights was to repel barbarian invaders from our shores, but from time to time a few left the Court to seek the Holy Grail. Before setting out on so perilous a quest the knights came to the remote, secluded, peaceful, wooded ravine of St Nectan's Glen, and prayed reverently, bowing their heads, resting solemnly on one knee, seeking divine guidance.

Even today the Glen retains its magical, mysterious qualities. It is named after a real saint, Nectan, who lived as a hermit here and may even have been a contemporary of Arthur. Like most of the Cornish saints, who included several of his brothers and sisters, he founded a chapel, this one on a pinnacle of rock above the spectacular, sixty-foot St Nectan's Kieve, a great smooth-sided cauldron of rock into which the water falls before flowing out and falling again through a natural arch. In the tower Nectan hung a silver bell, symbolically keeping alive the light of Christ. When local fishermen out at sea heard the bell ringing they knew that the saint was praying for their safety and looking after them, and even now when bad weather is approaching it is said that the residents of Tintagel can hear it tinkling. When weak and exhausted from his tireless work, he asked to be carried to a ledge above the waterfall and there dropped the bell into the clear waters of the Kieve, where it vanished from sight. Soon afterwards he died. Carefully, tenderly, his two sisters with whom he lived placed his body in an oak chest along with his personal sacrimental articles and a 'great treasure', though just what this consisted of we don't know. By miraculous means the ladies diverted the waterfall and buried Nectan under a great slab of rock in the bed of the pool where the waterfall ends after its 60 foot plunge, before the stream reverted to its natural course over his grave. True to his teachings, the ladies continued their reclusive lives at the chapel until they too died. Here too they were buried, and their grave is said to be under a flat stone near the foot of the waterfall, not far from that of Nectan. The story does not end here, however. To this day people have seen figures dressed like monks and heard sounds of music and chanting both in the Glen itself and on the road across it.

The story of Nectan's bell and treasure were not forgotten. Centuries later a group of local quarrymen set out to recover them, using their expertise and explosives to blast the Kieve. Just as they were about to fix the charges they all heard, clearly, the tinkling of a bell and a ghostly voice, "*The child is not yet born who shall recover this treasure*." The men stopped in their tracks. Collecting their equipment and tools they ran away as fast as they could. No other attempt has ever been made.

The Round Table plays a significant role in the tales of the Knights and their inspirational management by Arthur. Arthur built his Court on the basis of its shape, founding the Fellowship of the Knights with each member having a specific, designated place, neither above nor below that of his colleagues, emphasising their equality and ensuring that none should feel more important by sitting near near the head of the Table. But what happened to it after his death? Local folklore says it is underneath a circular mound of earth next to the Methodist Chapel at Bossiney. Nor has its power diminished over the centuries. Just as Arthur will return in the hour of England's need, so on Midsummer Night the Table rises with a flash, flooding the sky with golden light, then sinks again.

As with most Arthurian matters, even though we must accept that the real world of material fact is less potent than the myth, it is still a very good, fascinating tale.

WALK DIRECTIONS

Distance	4 miles	Time	3 hours
Map	OS Landranger 200 054885	Terrain	On both the outward and return sections of this walk there is a climb from almost sea level to 300 feet up steep steps. The richly wooded Rocky Valley and St Nectan's Glen are delightful but there are steps and it may be muddy.

Car parking Park in Tintagel, where there are several car parks.

>> Starting from the middle of the village follow the signs to 'Castle'.

>> Take the steep lane going down left marked 'Castle'. Cross the second footbridge across the stream, and carry on up the path which brings you to the outer wall. You can now walk through the castle ruins and down steep stairs, past large outcrops of rock, almost to sea level where you cross a bridge and begin the long climb up to The Island.

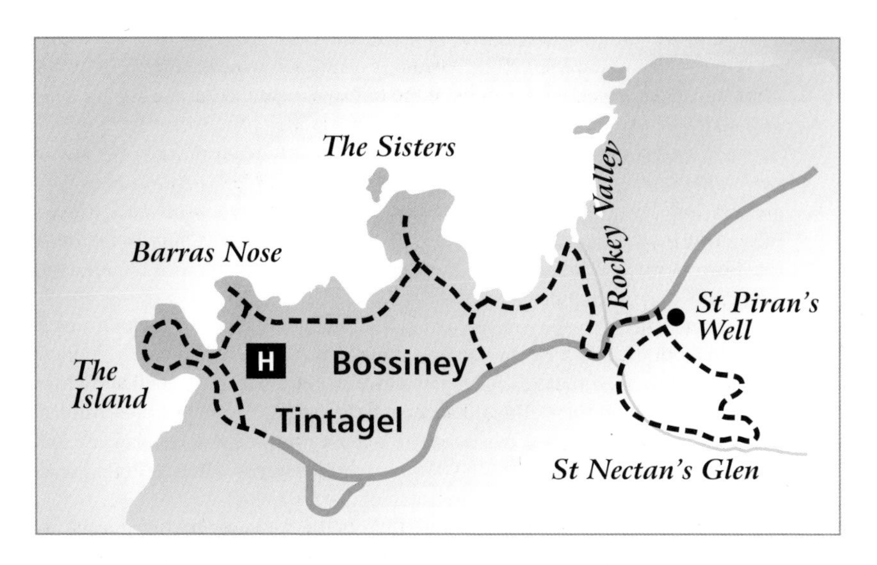

The significance of the route Uther Pendragon took into the castle is best appreciated at this point - which raises the strong likelihood that Geoffrey of Monmouth had actually been here or some-one had given him a very accurate description. To ease access for visitors this stretch has been made wider than in Geoffrey of Monmouth's time: if Gorlois returned he would need at least eight men to hold the path against Uther's army, instead of the three Geoffrey estimated. Many features claim Arthurian associations. 'King Arthur's Seat' is a natural notch in the slate cliff just below the southern edge of the plateau, and 'King Arthur's cups and saucers', some twenty small depressions two-six inches across. By the south-east corner of the chapel is 'King Arthur's Bed' and on a rock between the 'Seat' and the chapel, on the highest point of The Island's flat top, is 'King Arthur's Footstep', an artificial cavity in the life-sized shape of a human left foot, imprinted in the solid rock when he "... stepped at one stride across the sea." What further proof of Arthur's presence do you need? One theory is that in times past it featured in coronation ceremonies, with the newly-crowned monarch's foot firmly inserted in the footprint to symbolise his rule over the land.

>> You can walk round The Island on a number of paths. When you have recrossed the bridge and regained the castle proper you will come to 'King Arthur's Cove'.

>> Take the steps going down left to the beach. On your left, at the base of the headland directly below the castle, is 'Merlin's Cave'. Does it conjure up the place where in Tennyson's 'Idylls of the King' Arthur appears to Merlin after his secret early upbringing?

For there was no man knew from whence he came:
But after tempest, when the long wave broke
All down the thundering shores of Bude and Bos
There came a day as still as Heaven, and then

They found a naked child upon the sands
Of wild Dundagil by the Cornish sea;
And that was Arthur ...

It always seems strange to us that a powerful magician like Merlin should choose to live in such an uncomfortable, wet place as his cave pierces through the rock to connect small beaches on either side of the headland, and is filled by the sea at each high tide. Of course it is possible that Merlin used his skills to transform this unpromising habitation into a desirable residence. It must be said though that the cave's link with Merlin seems to be as recent as Victorian romantic imagination.

>> Go down to the beach and follow the signs for the Coast Path as it climbs away on your right. Where it splits in two, take the route bearing left.

>> Go past the side of the huge King Arthur's Castle Hotel, built in the 1890s by William Taylor, and which from a distance is sometimes mistaken by visitors for Tintagel Castle. The first headland you come to, Barras Nose, was used by Iron Age peoples to built their forts of banks and ditches, far older than the castle at Tintagel. It is the best place to savour the romance of the great headland opposite with its twelfth-century castle (and Arthur's if there ever was one). From the Coast Path you can see the famous gloomy cave of Barras Nose.

>> The path continues winding for another mile to the next headland, Willapark, with two small islands offshore, The Sisters.

On the north-east side of this headland a rough path drops to a large, grassy, detached mass: this is the dreaded Lye Rock on which many ships have met their end. It was the scene of a dramatic rescue in December 1893 when an Italian ship, 'Iota', was wrecked on it. At great personal risk local men saved the lives of seven of the crew but the rest were drowned including a young boy, Catanese Domenico, whose grave is in St Materiana's churchyard at Tintagel.

>> Continue to follow the path as it winds on and down from the neck of the headland, before descending steeply to a grassy bottom, which can be both muddy and difficult after rain. Go up the stone steps, helpfully set equally steeply in the turfy hillside, to a stile. The view ahead is of a series of succeeding headlands, with the sea beating precipitous flanks before pouring off rocky ledges. From here a rough track drops to the left to the beach at Bossiney Haven. Walk up the steep hill and into the village of Bossiney. The mound traditionally covering the Round Table is next to the Methodist Chapel, on the main road:

Hard by was great Tintagel's table round
And there of old the flower of Arthur's knights
Made fair beginning of a nobler time ...

>> To regain the Coast Path from the beach turn right up the track to the cliff top. Just before the gate opening onto the road at Bossiney turn left and skirt the coast. Continue to where the path falls sharply into the beautiful Rocky Valley, the lower, seaward part of St Nectan's Glen.

>> Do not go over the footbridge but turn right along the left bank of the wooded stream for about half a mile. Where the path bears left at the ruined buildings continue ahead for a few paces and look to your right for two labyrinth carvings cut into the rockface behind the fallen wall of the mill.

No-one knows what they signify or even their age: some say they are only a few centuries old, cut by a former owner of the mill, but they may be Bronze Age (c.

4000 years old) as the design appears in stone 'mazes' on the Scilly Isles, on isolated sites throughout the Celtic world and on Celtic jewellery. They are also the same design as the Glastonbury Tor maze so it is not surprising that people who believe in 'earth magic' find them full of meaning and power.

>> Continue along Rocky Valley, its small waterfalls and swirling pools interrupting the progress of the sparkling stream, until you cross a footbridge and emerge onto the road (B3263).

>> Turn left and walk along the road. Where it bears left turn right, signed for 'St Nectan's Glen', and in a few yards go past the holy well and chapel dedicated to St Piran. Turn right past the chapel and pass the houses before walking up another delightfully wooded valley. Bear right and follow the left-hand bank of the river, ignoring the first bridge but crossing the next two. You are now ascending as you continue past the ruined house, still bearing right, until you reach the fence. From here you can hear the tantalising sound of the waterfall before emerging at the Kieve, the traditional meeting place of the Knights of the Round Table. It must have been a damp home for a hermit!

Kieve is the Cornish word for cauldron, bowl or basin, aptly applied as the water drops 60 feet first into a granite basin then through a rocky cavity for its final fall into another rock basin and the river, a spectacular sight among overhanging trees and bushes.

As you stand and look, in this perfect setting for nymphs, it is interesting to compare and note the similarity of the saint's name, Nectan, to that of the old Celtic Water God, Nudd, Nodens or Nechtan.

>> Follow the path through the wood to join the road, where you turn left.

>> Return to Rocky Valley and continue over another wooden bridge and along the left bank of the stream as it heads to the coast. When the path forks go right to the end of the gorge to see where it joins the Atlantic in a series of cascades and falls. Return to the fork and follow the Coast Path waymark to your right.

>> At the next waymark you climb steeply out of the valley before descending steps to cross the access to Bossiney Cliffs. Continue ahead. Climb up the steps on the opposite side and cross the stile before descending yet again to a wooden footbridge and a sign for Willapark.

>> Continue along the Coast Path, climbing quite steeply before you emerge onto a grassy plateau. Here take the seaward path, bear right for a gap in the wall and then through a wooden kissing gate in the wall with the tall cliffs of Willapark on your right. This path leads to a small gap in the wall next to the sign for Barras Nose.

>> At Barras Nose ignore the footpath sign to Tintagel below the hotel and continue ahead around the coast, descending to cross the stream in front of Tintagel Head.

>> After crossing the stream, turn left inland, past the exhibition shop and go up the wide path back to Tintagel. At the road, turn right. On your left is The Great Hall of Chivalry, built in 1933 by Frederick Glasscock, to house a whose series of medievalised, fictitious Arthurian artefacts and scenes in stained glass and oils. From here, return to your car.

We do not leave King Arthur here. We will meet him again as he weaves his way through many of our tales and our walks, for this greatest of legends haunts every corner of Cornwall.

SLAUGHTERBRIDGE

KING ARTHUR'S LAST BATTLE

It is only four-and-a-half miles from Athur's legendary birth-place to where he supposedly led his Celtic forces in final battle sometime towards the middle of the sixth century. This short distance does not reflect the drama of his life between these two events.

For many years King Arthur ruled over his land. There was peace and prosperity. His knights travelled throughout the known world executing their many and various gallant deeds. But there came a time when Arthur's vision for Camelot began to crumble. Some knights left his service. Some died. Sir Lancelot betrayed him with his adulterous love for Queen Guinevere. Brooding over all, plotting his downfall, was his son, the traitorous, treacherous Mordred. Ever since he had been a young boy Mordred had been consumed by jealousy of Arthur, fed by the ambitious sorcery of his mother, Morgan le Fay. Now, finally, he determined to seize the throne and take the title of King of England for himself. He sought to fight and kill Arthur - nothing less would do.

For centuries the final struggle between Arthur and Mordred has been linked with 'Camlann'. *The Annales Cambriae*, probably put together in the ninth century, gave the date as AD 537. Geoffrey of Monmouth, knowing no more than any of his contemporaries where 'Camlann' might really be, located it at *Cambula*. Did he leave us with a clue, combining the two names of the River Camel which was formerly called the Alan? Historical doubts may exist about the location but cannot detract from the stirring brevity of the epic battle.

On the Monday after Trinity Sunday, Arthur was encamped by the infant River Camel. Opposing him were the hosts of Mordred. Here, according to the twelfth-century Worcestershire priest Layarmon,

> *... were gathered sixty thousand and more, Mordred was their leader. And the noble Arthur rode there with a huge army, although it was doomed.*

In those days armies didn't just charge into each other on horse and foot, slashing, hacking, thrusting. This was an age of chivalry and a date had to be agreed when the opponents should engage. But on the night before the proposed fight Arthur, restless, dreamt that the deceased Sir Gawaine stood by his bed, warning him against fighting that day for he would be killed and the battle lost. Arthur woke early in the morning and went straight to Mordred, who agreed to a postponement to the day following. They also agreed that if any knight on either side should draw his sword battle would commence. Unfortunately, later that same day, one of Arthur's knights was bitten by an adder and in an instantaneous, unthinking reaction drew his sword and killed it. That flash of iron was interpreted by Mordred's forces as a sign of betrayal and immediately charged towards Arthur's men. The two armies threw themselves on each other. Layarmon described how

> *On the River Camel they fought together, raised standards, massed them together, drew long swords and beat on the helmets. Sparks flew out, spears shattered, shields broke, shafts snapped. The mighty host fought together there. The Camel was in flood with measureless blood.*

For several hours the battle raged fiercely until only three knights were standing. Arthur was on the point of defeat. Sir Bedivere begged the king to leave while there was still time to regroup his exhausted men and fight another day. Arthur refused. He fought his way through the battlefield until he found Mordred. With a terrible cry, "*Traitor, now is thy death day come,*" he raised his huge spear and thrust it at Mordred, forcing it through his body "*more than a fathom*". The last scene, though, belongs to Sir Thomas Malory,

> *And when Sir Mordred felt that he had his death's wound he thrust himself with the might that he had up to the burr of King Arthur's spear, and right so he smote his father, King Arthur, with his sword holden in both hands, upon the side of the head, that the sword pierced the helmet and the tay of the brain and the noble Arthur fell in a swoon to the earth. And herewith Mordred dashed down stark dead to the earth.*

Grievously wounded, Arthur gave his final order. Sir Bedivere, now his last knight alive, returned the sword Excalibur to the Lady of the Lake, then carried the dying king to the seashore. Here a barge with six veiled, weeping women, bore him away to the island refuge "*in Avalon, with the fairest of all women*". There he died.

To this day the ancient, low, flat bridge is called Slaughterbridge, a name which conjures up some dreadful, blood-curdling event. But this is not the end of our story. Arthur's subjects were overcome with grief and erected a stone at the spot where he had slain his traitorous son Mordred, before succumbing to his own wounds. A few yards upstream from the bridge, half-hidden among the trees, encrusted with moss and now toppled over and embedded in the river bank, lies a large slab of granite.

Can we accept the claim that this nine-foot pillar in its dank and picturesque setting is really a memorial to that battle, or even marks Arthur's grave? It is a tombstone of the late sixth or seventh century. It is also inscribed. Though it is far from clear it is possible to discern 'CATIN (or LATINI) HIC IACIT FILIUS MAGARI' 'Catin (or Latinus) lies here, son of Magaris'. These final letters have been read as -ARI (as 'Atri', then'Atry') and since the sixteenth century have been interpreted as a contraction of the name ARTHUR, giving support to the 'Arthur' ascription. Sadly for those of us of a romantic nature that is unlikely.

In AD 814 Egbert collected the forces of Wessex, invaded Dumnonia and "*laid waste the land from east to west*", compelling its kings to pay him homage. Eleven years later the Cornish rebelled, only to be defeated again at 'Gafulford'. This is probably Camelford, and the name Slaughterbridge may commemorate Egbert's bloody victory rather than Arthur's last great battle. The stone itself is more likely to be a monument to another Celtic chieftain slain in that historic conflict around AD 825 during the Saxon conquest of Cornwall. Yet in popular lore this is Arthur's grave and always will be. Perhaps we can take heart from the epitaph which Malory gave him: *Hic iacet Arthurus, rex quandam rexque futurus*, 'Here lies Arthur, the once and future king', foretelling his return in Britain's hour of need.

Of course, many people deny that Arthur died after the battle of Camlann. They say he merely rests, ready to awake at the call. One of the places where he is supposed to be sleeping, surrounded by his knights in full armour, is King Arthur's Hall, not far from here on Bodmin Moor.

WALK DIRECTIONS

Distance	4½ miles (7.2km)	Time	2¼ hours
Map	OS Landranger 200 122854	Terrain	There is one steep descent/ascent on a road, otherwise moderate on paths through fields. One part is muddy and you will have to negotiate undergrowth and a stream.

Car Parking   Park at the junction of the A39 and the B3314, at Collan's Cross.

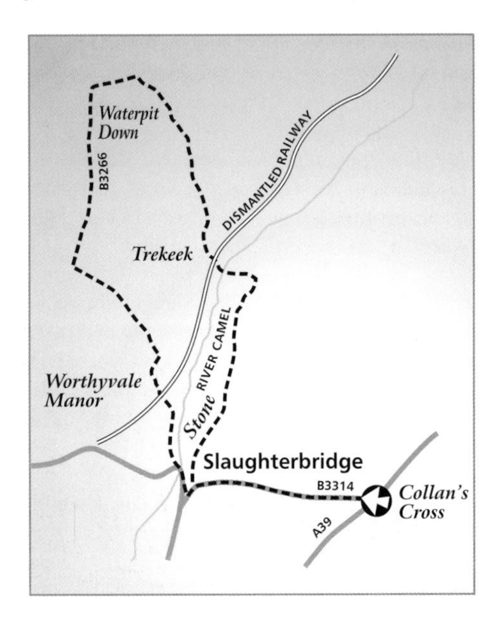

>> Follow the sign to Tintagel, walking down the steep, winding road (B3314). At the bottom of the hill the road turns sharply left and then right, where it crosses the infant River Camel over a low, flat bridge. This is the Slaughter Bridge, with its sign "King Arthur fought here in AD 575."
As you read this sign you are standing on the very spot where Arthur is said to have slain the traitorous Mordred, before being overcome by his own wounds.

>> At the side of the bridge is a stone gateway. Go through and after about 50 yards up the lane take the opening on your left by a large tree.

>> Cross this field to the bank of the stream, to where steps have been cut. You will need to clamber down them, but take care as they are old, worn and slippery, and the last few are made from roots of a tree. Now you must inch your way along the fern-draped stones at the edge of the stream to where, at the bottom, lying in the water, is Arthur's stone, neglected and uncared for but dignified and significant.
The stone is said to have stood originally on the main road by the bridge but later was laid in the river as a stepping stone. According to Lake's 'Parochial History' of 1867 the Lady Falmouth developed an interest in Arthurian matters and had it removed from the river bed and set up again by the side of the road. If this was so then the stone has travelled back into the water and further upstream. So not only its function but also its location are in doubt.

>> Climb back up the bank of the stream and return to the road. Turn right and bear left and where the road bends right take the signed footpath on your left through the field gate. From here walk diagonally right through two fields and cross the stile onto a lane.This leads you past Trevilla Park on your right and Grylls Rose on your left to Hendra.

>> Keep this property on your left and at the end of the garden turn sharp right onto the signed footpath. Within 200 yards (175m) bear left round the building and climb gently towards the gate at the top of the field. You emerge onto a lane, where you turn left. Go through Trekeek and continue to the junction with the road. Again turn left and walk to the junction with the main road (B3266).

>> Turn left and walk along this road for half a mile (.8km) before turning left onto the lane signed 'Worthyvale Manor'. Follow this lane as it bends to the right and then left, go over the railway again and rejoin the road (B3314) at Slaughterbridge.

>> If you wish to visit the Arthurian Museum, turn right and walk along the road. The museum is on your right in just over half a mile (.8km).

>> To return to your car turn left on the B3314, go over the Slaughter Bridge and retrace your steps up the steep road.

ST TEATH

ANNE JEFFERIES AND THE FAIRIES ...

In days gone by the daily lives of Cornish people were closely interwoven with another, more elusive population, the fairies. These were mischievous, teasing, laughing little sprites forever up to light-hearted practical jokes. Some say they came with the saints from Ireland, but no matter what their origin these friendly little things were ever ready to come into the homes of the sick, the old and the poor, bringing them wild flowers and entertaining them with old songs or dancing.

Times have changed. Few of us see them now because we are not out alone in the countryside when these enchanting creatures are around. We are also more sceptical. But just because we don't believe in them doesn't mean they have ceased to exist! They certainly do.

Anne Jefferies was born in St Teath in December, 1626, the daughter of a farm labourer. Her upbringing and early life were quite normal. In those days it was common around here for 'families of substance' to take the daughters of poorer folk into their household, feeding and clothing them until the age of 21 and training them to be useful maidservants. So when the time came Anne went into service with the family of Mr John Pitt, a wealthy yeoman of St Teath, and here she remained for the next few years. Again, she appeared to be quite ordinary, and along with the other girls of St Teath Anne was heading for a life of mundane routine as a dutiful wife, bringing up a clutch of children, attending church and being a valued member of her local community.

Along with every-one else the people of St Teath believed in the existence of fairies - and Anne's employers were no exception. They also knew that no matter whether they were a help or a hindrance, mischievous, playful or restless, it paid to keep on the right side of them. So when in 1645 the now 19-year-old Anne claimed she was in communication with local fairies not many eyebrows were raised - and certainly no alarm.

It was not unusual for Anne to spend time in her employer's garden, alone at her work. However, one day Mr Pitt found her there collapsed. When she regained consciousness she explained that she had been so frightened by six little folk, dressed in green, who had climbed over the hedge, that she went into some form of convulsion. From that day not only could she see and talk to the fairies but they gave her the ability to predict the future, to heal and even to become invisible herself.

For some time Anne was ill with 'distemper', but as her health improved so began her healing of others. The first time was when her own mistress, Mrs Pitt, injured her leg when out riding. Without any apparent prior knowledge Anne was able to say exactly where, when and how the accident had occurred, and by stroking the injured leg took all the pain away. When questioned, all she would say was that six 'persons' had told her - yet no-one had been to the house! Other successful cases followed. Word of Anne's abilities soon spread throughout the local countryside, and then further afield. Crowds of people, rich and poor, young and old, healthy and unwell, flocked to see her. She refused to accept any money and though she never bought any medicines or creams she always had them available, supplied secretly, she said, by her fairy friends. Moses Pitt, her employer's son, recorded how on occasions Anne would, incredibly, disappear and re-appear before his eyes or go without food for months on end, explaining only that the fairies brought her delicious meals.

However, trouble was brewing. Anne was too different from what people expected of servants. Some were jealous of her popularity or felt threatened. There were even whisperings that she was a witch. Knowing the only possible outcome of such accusations both the local vicar and the magistrates spoke to Anne, trying to convince her to stop all contact with the fairies. But the fairies knew what people were saying. That same evening when the Pitt family and Anne were sitting by the fire, the fairies called her away three times to warn her; they were deeply hurt and, strange as it seemed at the time, advised her when the time appeared right to quote from the Bible, the First Epistle of St John, chapter IV, verse I.

It was at this stage that the notorious John Tregeagle became involved. He issued an arrest warrant accusing Anne of witchcraft and communing with the Devil. In 1646 she was thrown into Bodmin Gaol. Tregeagle instructed the gaolers to put Anne in the worst part of the gaol and not to give her food, but despite being in prison for three months and the actual ill-treatment there was no deterioration in Anne's appearance or behaviour. The fairies supplied her with food every day and kept her company to cheer her up.

Fortunately for Anne the accusations did not withstand examination in court. Members of the Pitt family testified that she was a most trustworthy and reliable employee; others that her only motivation was to help people, never upsetting them; still others that though illiterate she was devout and well-versed in the scriptures. Her interrogators were further nonplussed when she quoted the Biblical text the fairies had told her. She was discharged from prison but her ordeal was not over as this was conditional upon her being kept under guard in Bodmin, where again John Tregeagle kept her without food.

After a time Anne was again brought before the court. This time no evidence was put forward and she was free to leave but as the Justices made a condition of her release that she should no longer live with the Pitt family, they arranged for her to take up service with a widowed relative, Mrs Frances Tom, near Padstow. Soon though she returned to her native St Teath to keep house for her brother, and while there she met and later married William Warren, a 'hind' or steward to a local physician. Anne Jefferies lived on, quietly doing her good work, looking after her husband, healing wherever she could. She was quite elderly when she died - and her secrets went with her to the grave.

WALK DIRECTIONS

Distance	5 ½ miles (8.9km)	Time	2½ hours
Map	OS Landranger 200 064806	Terrain	Quite easy along paths and roads but with two climbs past an ancient hillfort.

Car Parking Park outside the church

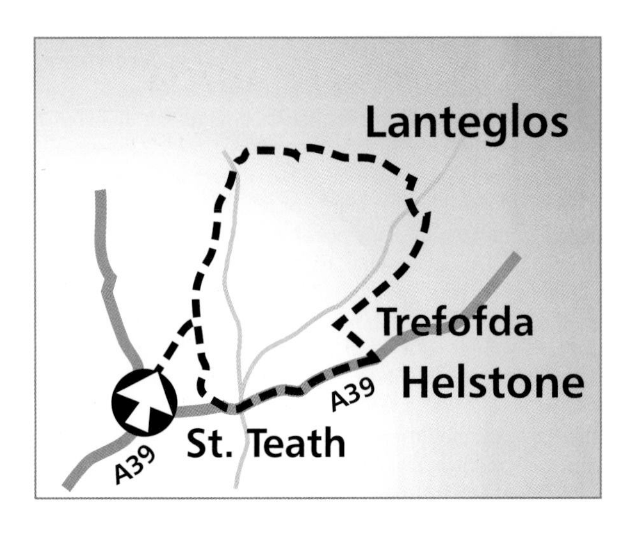

>> From the church walk down the slight hill to the road. Turn left onto the B3267, signed 'Westdowns', and pass the houses on both sides of the road. Just before you get to the public house look for the footpath sign on your right, and go between the houses and over the stile into the field. Now walk straight ahead, over another stile and through another field to the gate from which you emerge onto a metalled lane.

>> Turn left and walk along this lane until you reach Newhall Manor. At the crossroads go straight over onto the public footpath which leads you along the right hand side of the Manorhouse and then over a stile, across a field and via a gate into a copse. Several other paths join the one you are on, one from the right and one from the left, but you keep walking on the central path to the gate on your right. Go through and then walk straight ahead through the fields to the unsurfaced lane.

>> Turn left and within a few yards take the public footpath on your right, over a stile, signed 'Ancient Settlement'. Keep on this path, climbing steadily and passing Castle Goff hillfort on your right. At the stile you emerge onto a surfaced road. Turn right and follow this road until it forks. Take the left fork and at the junction turn left, signed 'Lanteglos'. Walk past the church on your right and immediately take the public footpath signed on your right. Now you begin to descend along the contour of the hill through fields to the hamlet of Trefofda. Go through the gate onto the road and take the gate immediately on your left, from where you descend and head for a house slightly to your right. At the gate you emerge onto the A39.

>> Walk alongside this road to its junction with B3267 and bear right, signed 'St Teath'. Continue on this road until immediately after the second property on your right, turn right onto the footpath over a stile.

>> Keep on this footpath to Trevilley Farm and when you pass the buildings and the farmhouse, turn left down its drive. Where this joins the lane go straight across and over the stile onto the footpath. Turn left.

>> You are now retracing your steps from earlier in the walk and this will lead you into St Teath. Go through the houses and when you join the road turn left. The church is on your right, as is your car.

BODMIN MOOR

THE RETURN OF EXCALIBUR ...

There is something mysterious about deep, still waters which stirs our imagination. One of the county's strangest phenomena and one of its only two natural freshwater lakes (Loe Pool is the other), Dozmary Pool, a sheet of moorland water in a windswept natural basin set high in the austere landscape, its outline broken only by the occasional clump of reeds or withered thorn bush, has long been associated with ancient beliefs. How does it exist? No stream flows into it; there are no obvious springs; it drains no part of the Moor. One legend says it has an underground connection with the sea, and certainly its name means 'drop of sea', so perhaps in ancient times it was considered a symbolic entrance to the Underworld. For centuries it was thought to be bottomless, and though in 1533 it was reported to be about fourteen fathoms deep and in 1859 actually dried up, these facts did nothing to dispel the belief. It is also the nearest lake to Slaughterbridge.

As King Arthur lay fatally wounded by his son Mordred, he ordered Sir Bedivere to take the magical sword Excalibur to a mysterious lake and cast it into the water. When he arrived "*by zig-zag paths, and juts of pointed rock*", according to Tennyson, at "*the shining levels of the lake*" Sir Bedivere couldn't bring himself to carry out the task.

He gazed so long, as he stood ...
... but at the last it seem'd
Better to leave Excalibur conceal'd
There in the many-knotted waterflags,
That whistled stiff and dry about the marge.
So strode he back to the wounded king.

Arthur repeated his order. Again Sir Bedivere was unable to do it. Finally, Sir Bedivere realised that his task had a deeper, mystical significance than he could comprehend, so for the third time he returned to the lake. Now he

... plunged
Among the bulrush-beds, and clutch'd the sword,
And strongly wheel'd and threw it. The great brand
Made lightnings in the splendour of the moon ...
... So flash'd and fell the brand Excalibur:
But ere he dipt the surface, rose an arm
Clothed in white samite, mystic, wonderful,
And caught him by the hilt, and brandish'd him
Three times, and drew him under the mere.

The sword which the Lady of the Lake had given Arthur vanished into the deep waters as mysteriously as it had come. Dozmary Pool is said to be that lake.

What, asks the cynic, was a magical sword doing in water in the first place, and why should it be returned to the Lady of the Lake? This is one part of the legend of Arthur that historical research can substantiate. Ponds, pools and meres were sacred to Iron Age society. A still water's surface was the only place you could see the reflection of your face. It was a mirror to the Other-world, the world of spirits, of the dead - for your reflection was not you but an

Other-world version of you. Death was marked by placing the deceased's possessions in water. Excalibur may not have risen from the lake on a mystic arm but more likely than not would have have been put there after a chieftain's death.

Other ghosts are present here, too. The Pool is a meeting place of the Wild Hunt, a pack of spectral hounds, and is visited by a wraith-like hound known as the Barguest. Some people have actually witnessed a shadowy coach and horses driving round and round the lake, and then driving into it; others have seen flitting lights kindled in places where no human could possibly go.

Even that is not the end. Here is one of the many haunts of the wicked John Tregeagle, the infamous Cornishman who sold his soul to the devil. He returned from the dead and various ways were devised to keep him busy, one of which was emptying Dozmary Pool for all eternity using only a cracked, leaking limpet shell. Now the winds howling across Bodmin Moor carry a sinister message more chilling even than the iciest north-eastern blast as they rattle the panes of moorland farms, for these sounds are the howls of anguish of Tregeagle's spirit as his black soul is doomed to wander for ever.

WALK DIRECTIONS

Distance	3 miles	Time	2½ hours
Map	OS Landranger 201 193746	Terrain	Flat, largely a road walk, but can be muddy in parts.

Car parking: Park on the roadside immediately opposite Jamaica Inn's car park.

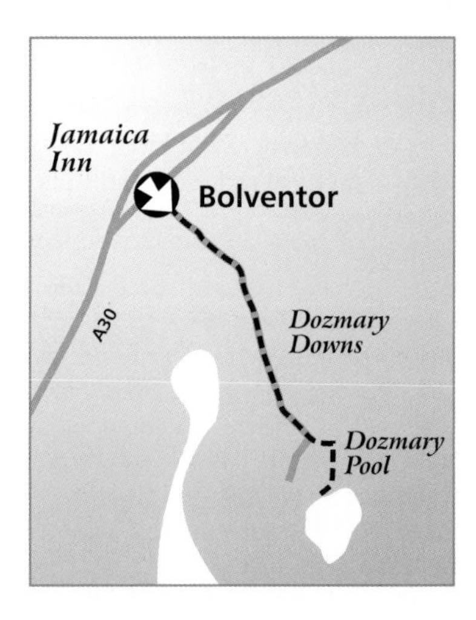

>> Walk along the lane opposite the Inn, signed to 'Dozmary Pool'. Once you get beyond the cattle grid the Moor opens up and you begin to feel the freedom of its broad expanse.
Away to your right is a stretch of water, part of the man-made Colliford Lake. From now on you will see cattle grazing: it is interesting to note how many of them are black, like the peat of the moor itself.

>> After about 1¼ miles the road is unfenced and swings to the right. On the bend take the track on your left signed 'Footpath to Dozmary Pool'. Now you can appreciate these wide Bodmin skies and its distinctive light. Suddenly before you lies one of the great jewels of Cornwall, a lonely expanse of water. The fact that it is so high on the Moor is one of its strange features.
It is a lake of many moods. When placid it is like a mirror as it reflects the surrounding moorland and the sky. On a sunny day it sparkles, washing on the reeds. In melancholy mood it can be dark and threatening, black from the peat below the surface. It is always mysterious and magical. Stand here in the twilight when the wind is howling, driving dark clouds across the moorland sky, and can you deny Dozmary's claim to hold the secret of the resting place of mighty Excalibur, which Arthur himself wielded to such effect? Can you make out Sir Bedivere in the mist, casting the sword to the Lady of the Lake? Is it a trick of light, or did you see those finger-tips breaking the surface?
It is easy to imagine that all the lore is true - a very strange place where even the least imaginative of us would invent it if the lake was not already haunted by the ghost of John Tregeagle.

>> The Pool can be circumnavigated with care, though it is rather marshy.

>> Return to your starting point and then back to Bolventor and your car.

... AND THE HURLERS

This is a unique if bleak landscape of the ancient intermixed with relics of an industrial past, shaped by places of ritual and the necessities of survival. On desolate, mist-shrouded Bodmin Moor, its few trees bent by the wind that "*tyrannizes ... rowling upon the high hills and moors in furious gusts*," as a Tudor writer put it, we can delve into the pre-history of our island. Here are extensive barrows, massive chambered tombs, enigmatic stone circles, giant, leaning standing stones, Bronze Age hut settlements built long before the Romans or the Celtic saints arrived. Simultaneously we can be brought nearer to our time by the decaying ivy-clad Victorian engine-houses and disused quarries, for centuries after those prehistoric peoples the place was teeming with miners and quarrymen searching for copper, lead and usable granite.

On the south-eastern edge of Bodmin Moor are three inter-locking rings of standing stones, their centres lying along a straight line, which have been dated to the Bronze Age, around 1500 BC. In the outer rings only a handful of the stones remain upright, and a few lie where they have fallen over, overgrown with moss and heather. Most of those in the middle circle are still standing at regular intervals. Together the three groups of hunched shapes are certainly mysterious. What was their significance? Although the stones were placed with considerable precision, which must have involved enormous effort, energy and manpower, no-one is sure why they were erected or what strange ceremonies were acted out here. We know the answer. It has been handed down to us in folklore.

Hurling was a once a popular game, played by virtually every red-blooded Cornish male. According to eye-witness accounts it was a savage free-for-all in which men of rival villages vied to knock a ball through goals often placed several miles apart. Richard Carew in his

Survey of Cornwall published in 1602, described it:
The ball in this game may be compared to an infernal spirit; for whosoever catcheth it fareth straightways like a madman, struggling and fighting with those about to hold him; and no sooner is the ball gone from him but he resigneth his fury to the next receiver and himself becometh peaceable as before.

One day many years ago, a group of men were hurling right here, unconcerned that this was on a Sunday. Their noisy laughter and vigorous activity did not go unnoticed. In a startling flash of light the teams of men were frozen in granite exactly where they stood. This was divine punishment for abusing the Sabbath. Presumably there must have been three games going on simultaneously as there are three stone circles, and to look at them the men must have practised a particularly sedate version of the game - but ever since these rings of stones have been known as The Hurlers. The lore is obviously of long standing, as in the eighteenth century William Borlase scornfully dismissed it: "*The stones by the vulgar are supposed to have been once men and thus transformed for their hurling upon the Lord's Day*." He thought the circles were Druid's temples. By the way, there is no point trying to count the stones: tradition says it is impossible to arrive at the same number twice!

To the west of the circles are two outlying standing stones, called the Pipers who were men making music while the hurling was going on - and met the same fate. It really was unfortunate as their only crime was to be supporting their teams that day!

But back to our original question: did these stone circles fulfil an important role in the prehistoric society which placed them with such care? Alignments to sun and moon at significant points in their annual cycle suggest the site may have figured in ceremonies to mark and celebrate the natural rhythms of life. It would be difficult of course to use the stone circles as observatories with any accuracy, so their alignments were symbolic rather than scientific. That they are close to other ritual sites in a 'ceremonial landscape' suggests they provided a sacred space distinct from the mundane everyday world in which the dramas of prehistoric religion and ceremonial were played out for the benefit of the wider population. So examine the landscape around you. While you stand at the Hurlers, look 120 degrees to the east towards Caradon Hill, and here six hundred yards away is a cairn group; then look in the opposite direction and again six hundred yards away you are in perfect alignment to the Craddock Moor stone circle, followed by Embanked Avenue with its group of cairns, and then Stone Row, one of several such rows on Bodmin Moor. Curious or merely coincidental?

From the Hurlers the northern horizon is dominated by the stony ramparts of the Neolithic hilltop settlement on Stowe's Hill, and Rillaton Barrow, the second largest cairn on the moor, sits on top of a ridge on the near horizon. Do such 'landmark alignments' have astronomical significance? From the Craddock Moor stone circle the sun rises over Stowe's Hill at the midsummer solstice and on that same date from the Leaze circle it rises over Garrow Tor. Goodaver stone circle stands on a ridge in the centre of Bodmin Moor: from here the summer sun sets over the summit of Brown Willy, and the equinox sun rises over Kilmar Tor and sets over Hawk's Tor - all significant horizon features.

The Hurlers are not the only interesting stones here. In appearance that curious but natural granite formation known as the Cheesewring is so odd, its seven slabs set one on the other with the smaller stones at the bottom, spreading into a bulbous middle, then lessening in size

ST. NECTAN'S KIEVE

LABYRINTH AT ROCKY VALLEY

TINTAGEL CASTLE

THE HURLERS, BODMIN MOOR

DOOM BAR, HAWKERS COVE, PADSTOW

SLAUGHTER BRIDGE

again at the top, standing over twenty feet tall in total, that people have been convinced it must have been a direct result of the Deluge. Did you know that the top stone turns three times when it hears a cock crowing at a nearby farm?

In ancient times a Druid priest lived at Rillaton, just to the south. He used to sit on the rocks at a place still known as Druid's Chair, offering refreshing wine from a golden goblet to passing travellers and weary huntsmen. But this was no ordinary cup. However many drank, it never emptied. One day a group of hunters passed by after chasing a wild boar across nearby Trewartha Marsh. With more bravado than common sense one of them boasted that he could empty the cup. Snatching it, he drank and drank without having any effect on its contents until, increasingly inebriated as well as annoyed, he threw the wine into the Druid's face, leapt onto his horse and rode away as fast as he could. Anger and wine had their effect and the horse slipped over a rock outcrop, killing both itself and its rider. When his colleagues caught up they buried him where he had fallen, still holding the goblet. That might have been the end of the story but in 1837 excavations at Rillaton Barrow unearthed a skeleton, some Bronze Age pottery, a bronze dagger - and a priceless golden goblet! The Rillaton Cup is now in the British Museum but you can see a replica in the Royal Cornwall Museum, Truro.

WALK DIRECTIONS

Distance 7½ miles Time 3½ hours
Map OS Landranger 201 260711 Terrain Easy moorland walking with two climbs.
Car parking: Park in the public car park at the western end of Minions, west of B3254.

Minions is an unusual name, perhaps called after a Celtic ruler who lived sometime in the Dark Ages. At 1034 feet (304m) above sea level, it is also Cornwall's highest village, which in its Victorian boom years was the focal point for 4,000 miners. Interestingly a river rises here. The River Smeaton leaves this bare plateau to its rendezvous with the sea near Looe.

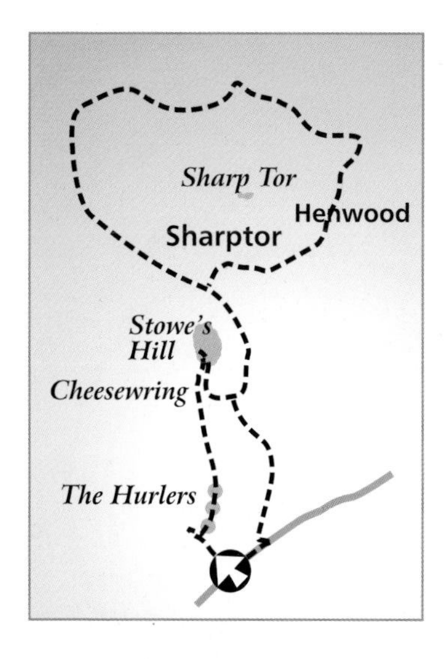

>> Take the track on your left, signed to 'The Hurlers', which leads onto the moorland. Continue until you reach the Information Board on your right, facing the Hurlers stone circles. The twin Pipers stand together on the right of the track.

>> Walk through the circles, heading north-west towards the rocky hill in the near distance. Pass the large rocks and scattered slabs of stone, all with wedge and groove markings, which are detritus of nineteenth-century quarrying.

>> As you get near to the hill on the southern edge of a quarry look out for a small cave slightly to your left, its opening directly onto the moor.

Daniel Gumb, a stone cutter and self-taught mathematician and astronomer, lived with his wife and nine children in a cave in the 1730s. He himself lived in it until his death. This one is a smaller reconstruction which was moved 100 yards (90m) to the south-west when, sadly, the main cave was destroyed as quarrying operations reached the original location in the nineteenth century. Daniel had carved his name and the date, 1735, in the granite as well as geometrical shapes, one of which was the proof of Pythagoras's theorem. His fine carving and the epitaph he composed for himself can be seen at Linkinhorne church nearby:

'Here I lie by the churchyard door;
Here I lie because I'm poor.
The further in, the more you pay,
But here I lie as warm as they.'

>> Keeping to the left of the cave take the path past the quarry to the Cheesewring.

Its name derives from its close resemblance to a cider press, with round, flat stones to squeeze the juice from apple pulp, known as 'cheese'. It was formed partly by weathering but also by the cooling, layer by layer, of liquid granite as it welled up from the depths of the Earth, creating this strange effect of slabs balanced one on the other.

>> Follow the path ahead to the summit of Stowe's Hill, a site of prehistoric importance.

Much of the summit is surrounded by a line of rocks, piled up. These have nothing to do with Cheesewring Quarry but are survivors of Stowe's Pound, one of several Iron Age hillforts around the edge of the Moor where the ingenious builders were able to use the natural rock formations and contours as an integral part of the defences.

Just below the main summit pile of boulders is the Devil's Chair - whoever sits in it becomes a poet or goes mad!

There are magnificent views from here, but look south-eastwards to a mound on top of a low hill in the middle distance, between Stowe's Hill and the village of Minions. This mound shelters Rillaton Barrow, where the gold goblet was found.

>> Leave the hill by taking the path downwards next to the fence on the south side of the quarry, heading for the track on the left which lies between the two fenced-off areas at the base of the Pound.

The granite sleepers you can see are all that is left of the Liskeard and Caradon Railway, which from 1877 took granite from Stowe's Pound to Looe where it was shipped to London and elsewhere.

>> Turn left and skirt North Wadbrook Farm by the gate on the right of the farmhouse. At the next gate continue straight on, through another gate and along the bed of the Kilmar Railway as it curves right. Just beyond is a stone-built loading ramp, where you turn left.

>> Now head south-east towards Bearah Tor Ridge and then down to Bearah Tor Quarry, following the track to the lane by Blackcoombe Farm where you turn right and head towards Henwood village. When you reach the village telephone box take the lane on your right signed 'Sharptor' and 'Minions'. Walk up the hill and take the lane on your right, climbing steeply past the cottages. When you reach the gate 325 yards (300m) before Wadbrook Farm, take the track on your left. You begin by doubling back on the lane but as you join the tramway with its granite sleepers you bear to the right, following the contour of the hill.

>> You now join a wider track on the left and continue down towards Minions.

By the house in the trees is a former mine building, South Phoenix Mine, which was built in 1881 and restored in 1991 to house an exhibition of the history of mining in the area. The Caradon Mines were the centre of the nineteenth-century copper boom, but also produced large quantities of tin, employing hundreds of men, women and children.

>> Follow the path on the right side of the building, past the house and into the car park. Turn right along the road, through the village, and return to your car.

ST BREOCK

WICKED JOHN TREGEAGLE

When the wind howls over the moors - that is John Tregeagle's tortured soul calling as it flees the pursuing Devil and his hellish hounds. When the pale moon is shining and dogs bark their warning - that is John Tregeagle's spirit disturbing them. When the sea turns black as night and waves move threateningly to the shore - that is John Tregeagle's spirit trying to escape its labours. The infamous bogeyman permeates every corner of Cornwall.

Although he was a real live person, there is little to find of him. The Tregeagle family mansion was at Trevorder, but this burned down in the nineteenth century and was rebuilt on a smaller scale before becoming a working farm.

The church has slate and brass memorials to those Tregeagles but there is none to John - and strangely the pages in the parish register which bore his signature and recorded his death have been removed. His reputation reputation rests on the extent to which he was hated for his ruthlessness.

John was born around 1638 in Bodmin, the only child of a yeoman. Even as a schoolboy he was different: thin and pale, unsociable - and cruel. At the age of 14 his father apprenticed him to an attorney, Mr Pendennis, in the High Street, and young John soon excelled at the work, running errands, tidying the office and maintaining ledgers so well that when the cashier retired he was promoted. It wasn't long before he began to increase his wages by helping himself to the petty cash. But to him the most exciting part of his job was to attend the magistrates' court where he could watch criminals be given harsh punishments.

Following the Duke of Monmouth's rebellion in 1685, 'the hanging judge', Judge Jeffreys, took the Western Circuit and when he came to Bodmin John watched how his inhumanity made a mockery of justice. John became one of the Judge's informers. Amongst other fabrications, he claimed that his employer, Mr Pendennis, was sympathetic to the rebellion and that he and his wife were engaged in treasonable activities, but before they could be brought before the Lord Chief Justice and the hangman could have his way, they committed suicide. In return Jeffreys arranged for Tregeagle to be appointed as a magistrate and take over ownership of all the Pendennis property. Now John's true motives came to the fore. No-one who came before him in court was safe and his 'justice' was designed to increase his own power and wealth. He deprived farmers of their land and turned them from their homes, unconcerned that many died of hunger and exposure in the following winters.

Then he plotted to marry sixteen-year-old Rachel, a daughter of Trelawney Polgreen of Tehidy Manor, a wealthy and successful mine-owner. To do this he made a contract with the Devil. Make no mistake, he was a willing recruit. Tregeagle was to have Rachel Polgreen and the Tehidy estates. The Devil was to have his soul. The mechanics were simple: Tregeagle was to play cards with Polgreen and the Devil would ensure he always won. Over several nights Trelawney Polgreen lost his entire estate, farms and mansion, lock, stock and barrel, until he had only one thing left: he wagered the hand of his daughter against what was now Tregeagle's fortune. Crafty as ever, Tregeagle demanded a signed deed to confirm this promise - at which Polgreen had a heart attack and fell to the floor, dead. Was everything he had worked for to be snatched away? Together, he and the Devil forged Polgreen's signature. The day after Polgreen's funeral, Tregeagle arrived to take possession. Rather than agree, Rachel stabbed herself to death with a pair of scissors. Tregeagle took the estate.

People were aghast at what had happened to such a prominent family, and Tregeagle was charged with forgery. He pleaded innocence and called the Devil himself as a witness. In a flash of thunder and foul smoke, there stood the Prince of Darkness, and he persuaded the lawyers to find Tregeagle guilty so he could have his soul. The judge was on the point of pronouncing the death sentence when the Devil took Tregeagle's soul from his body but with an unearthly shriek it squirmed from the Devil's grasp and fled. From that day to this it rushes impulsively over the rocks and gorse of the moors, the Devil in hot pursuit.

Many other stories have been attributed to John Tregeagle during his lifetime, and afterwards. In one, he murdered his first wife and children, then married a succession of heiresses, murdering each in turn to get their money. In another, a dispute arose between two wealthy families over the ownership of extensive lands around Bodmin. This was complicated by Tregeagle having acted for one of the claimants, destroying old deeds and forging others, and selling large portions of the land, misappropriating all the money. It was only after Tregeagle's death that these transactions came to light. Again the two families sought ownership but just as the Judge was about to sum up the final hearing the defendant called a last witness - and a throb of chilling terror went through the court as the ghost of John Tregeagle took the witness stand. It was clear from its cross-examination that the defendant had been victim of a complex system of fraud.

Now, the punishments. So wicked had he been that even death had little effect. Just before he died, John, in his capacity as Justice of the Peace, had been witness to a large loan. When time came for repayment the debtor denied he had taken it out and when Bodmin Court was told the transaction had been witnessed replied that Tregeagle should swear to it before the bench - thinking that would be the end of the matter. Now calling John Tregeagle from the grave was not a wise thing to do. His spirit had been waiting for just such an opportunity. With a frightening flash Tregeagle's ghost appeared in the witness box. Seething with unearthly rage the ghost threw itself onto the now terrified defendant. Fortunately the man was experienced in magical matters: though badly shaken, he snatched up a newborn child whose innocence kept the evil spirit at bay. Court practices must have been different in those days for the jury took all this in their stride, found the defendant 'not guilty' and added a plea on behalf of the ghostly Tregeagle for his co-operation.

Now the man had to find a way to keep Tregeagle's ghost away from him permanently. First he employed a local vicar to exorcise the ghost, but this was unsuccessful. Next the clergy debated how they could save Tregeagle's soul, and concluded that as the Devil found work for idle hands it must be given a task difficult beyond human abilities that would last for ever. Their scheme met these criteria: issued with a cracked, leaking limpet shell, Tregeagle was banished to Dozmary Pool and ordered to empty it, a task that would earn penance for his sins and take all eternity. To make sure he didn't shirk they arranged for a pack of headless hounds to guard him. Year after year, Tregeagle bent over the dark water, labouring hard but making no impression on the level of the pool. This was all watched by the Devil. Should Tregeagle falter in his appointed task, the Devil could seize him. Storms were conjured up and summer heat blistered down, but still Tregeagle worked on. Until during one mighty tempest Tregeagle had had enough and ran. Crowds of demons were at his heels. Three times he scampered over the gorse and rocks round the lake and three times they followed him.

On he fled to Roche Rock pursued by the baying hounds of Hell, intent on seeking sanctuary in the hermit's cell perched on the summit. Nearer and nearer came the thwarted spirits as he scrambled up the crag and thrust his head through the tiny east window but leaving his body exposed to their fangs. Week after week Tregeagle writhed and shrieked as the hermit prayed to be relieved of his sinful visitor and the demons who swarmed around. Tregeagle howled to such an extent that none of the local people dared go near the place and no inhabitant of the moors or neighbouring towns slept a wink at night. Not, that is, until a priest from a near-by church came to the rescue and by some further powerful spell Tregeagle was wafted away to a lonely beach on the north coast near Padstow where he was set another hopeless task: making trusses of sand and plaiting ropes to bind them at the edge of the sea.

His existence was one of futile toil. His despairing cries were dreadful and continuous as each recurring tide destroyed his work. He was no more welcome at Padstow than at Roche so St Petroc removed the spirit in chains which he had himself forged with prayer. This time Tregeagle was banished to Bereppa, now condemned to carry sacks of sand across the estuary of the River Cober and empty them at Porthleven until the beach was cleared down to the flat rocks. The wily saint knew that the sweep of the tides here would carry the sand back as quickly as it was removed. Long and in vain did Tregeagle labour. One day as he was wading heavily-laden across the estuary one of the watching hounds of Hell made him drop a huge sack which blocked off the river. There, to this day, rests the bar of sand, Loe Bar. Since the harbour at the estuary was now ruined the locals were as distressed and angry as had been the Padstow folk. Now Tregeagle was sent to sweep the sands of Porthcurno Bay round the Tol-pedn-Penwith until he had covered the rocks at Nanjizal Bay. When you walk this rugged headland you will appreciate the magnitude of the task. At certain tides these bars vanish and re-appear at other parts along the cliff base. Then they re-appear. If you stand on the cliffs you will hear wheeling seabirds and the thunder of Atlantic breakers - and Tregeagle's terrifying, menacing screams. He is still labouring here, still bellowing in fury above the wind, his roarings predicting approaching storms.

In reality John Tregeagle worked for John, Earl of Radnor as steward of Lanhydrock. In this capacity the historic John seems to have been a thoroughly unpleasant character who thought nothing of having folk arrested on false charges in order to seize their possessions, or growing rich by cheating them, but if he actually accomplished even a small proportion of the dreadful things credited to him either he was a man of frenetic energy or he made little time for his more orthodox activities on the estate.

It appears that towards the end of his life Tregeagle regretted his pact with the Devil. He had become very wealthy and now used money from his ill-gotten gains to bribe the vicar to bury him in consecrated ground amongst his predecessors here at St Breock. It was not to last. A later vicar had his body exhumed and discarded, and now no-one knows where he rests. Or is that because he doesn't rest at all? Some say he became a huge bird luring travellers to their deaths on Bodmin Moor, others that he swoops around the cliffs of Land's End as a giant gull, still others that his soul flits eternally over St Breock Downs. Beware!

WALK DIRECTIONS

Distance	3¼ miles (5.3km)	Time	2 hours
Map	OS Landranger 200 998725	Terrain	Easy through fields and a short stretch of minor roadway, with one steep but short climb in a wooded valley.

Car Parking Park in the central car park, Wadebridge

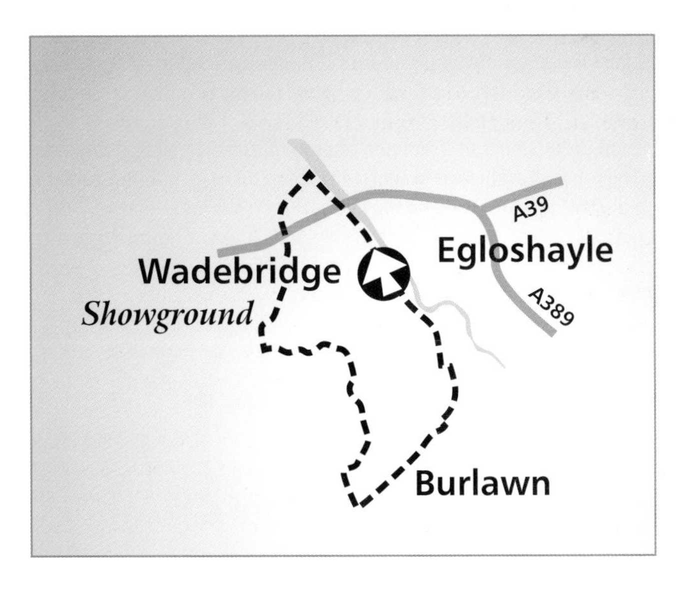

>> Leave the car park at the far end from the entrance and walk through the enterprise park buildings until you reach the River Camel. Turn left along the metalled road. Go past the sewage works where the road becomes a wide track and turn left to climb up the hill to Trevanson.

>> Go into the hamlet, passing the farm and houses, and go over the signed stile on your left of the gate, continuing ahead through more houses.

>> At the minor road continue up the hill to the junction with the main road, A39. Take the underpass and go over the stile. Continue in the same direction and when you see a gate on your left walk for about another 150 yards (130m) and go across the stile in the hedge. Keep walking in the same direction and across another stile. Now head for the stile at the corner of the field, go over and, keeping the hedge to your right, and when you arrive at the bottom of the field go down the steps, where you emerge onto a road.

>> Turn right and walk to the T-junction, passing the cottages. At the junction continue straight ahead down the lane on the left-hand side of the former rectory. Walk past the cottages and through the wrought-iron entrance to St Breock church. *The Tregagle Aisle, or St Michael's Chapel, contains memorials to a number of families, including the Tregeagles. Arthur Mee wrote of John Tregeagle:*

> *"Here lies the wicked steward who ground the faces of the poor, Jan Tregeagle ... They say his memory flits about St Breock Downs for he sold his soul to the devil, and his uneasy spirit was doomed to spin ropes of sand and bail out bottomless pools with a leaking limpet shell."*

>> From the church entrance gates turn right and go down the hill. Keep on the road as it bears right, and just a few yards after crossing the bridge over the stream take the stile on your left. Cross the field diagonally left upwards but keeping the boundary on your right, heading for the gate at the top.

>> When you emerge onto the road turn left and walk along it to the village of Polmorla. At the T-junction turn right and at the cross-roads keep walking straight ahead. Walk over the bridge over the stream and bear right and then left. Take the first footpath on your right at Treneague and follow it to Trevorder, at one time the family home of the Tregeagles.

>> Continue to the road where you turn left, signed 'Burlawn', go over the cross-roads and at a sharp left-hand turn with a house facing you, take the public footpath to its left.

>> Descend on this path to Treraven where you turn left onto a minor road. Very shortly you turn right onto a footpath which takes you to the bank of the River Camel. Bear left and walk to the car park.

PADSTOW

THE DOOM BAR ...

The River Camel begins at a spring on Hendra Burnick Down, high above Camelford. As a tiny stream it trickles across a harsh, soggy landscape, its few trees bent by the prevailing wind, on its meandering journey to join the Atlantic. Near its mouth lies Padstow. Records show that this has been a port since before the sixteenth century but it is now bedevilled by the notorious Doom Bar, that great, grim sandbank stretching across the river which prevents shipping of any considerable size from using the natural harbour.

When the harbour was deep and open it was a mermaid's playground. Unlike many of her kind she was a friendly creature and she guarded Padstow. A young local sailor had bought a gun to shoot birds and small animals, and one day, looking for something different to shoot, made his way to the Camel estuary. There he saw a girl sitting on a seaweed-covered rock surrounded by a pool, with her back to him as she absent-mindedly combed her flowing, long hair. The man crept up behind her, saw her reflection in the pool - and recognised just how beautiful her face and golden locks really were.

She too saw his reflection and turned. They spoke for some time and the man became so enchanted that he asked her for a lock of hair and to marry him. Rather curtly, she refused both, warning him not to harm her or she would curse the town. Nonetheless, angry at being spurned, he raised his gun and fired. As she tried to protect herself she pulled herself out of the pool and exposed the glittering scales of a fish tail. The man was terrified. He had shot a mermaid. As a sailor he knew this was a bad omen. The mermaid dived but quickly re-appeared, and as she died she retaliated by throwing a handful of sand at him. Thus was created the Bar. She cursed the estuary, promising this sand would prove a doom to ships and their crew, and many lives would be lost. Then she fell back into the pool, her blood staining the water.

How right she was. As the young sailor walked back from Hawker's Cove the sea began to moan. That very night a ferocious gale blew up and only when it had subsided did the Padstow townsfolk leave their homes to check on the damage: and now gazed on a huge sand bar which stretched across the mouth of the estuary from Hawker's Cove to the opposite bank at Daymer Bay, restricting the entrance to their previously safe harbour. That was not all. It was already littered with broken ships. As the waves rose and curled a wailing cry could be heard above the thundering of the tide. Ever since, whenever a ship is wrecked on Doom Bar and men are drowned, the mermaid's cry echoes across the estuary.

Doom Bar is appropriately named. It may provide shelter from the Atlantic swell for today's sailor but is a mixed blessing. In less than a square mile of sea some 300 vessels, 3 lifeboats and 150 victims have been lost here in the last 150 years. Along this inhospitable north coast there is no other harbour of any size from Hartland to Newquay, and neither of these offer a haven in a northerly gale or at low tide. Consequently, vessels caught in foul weather have tried to gain the refuge of the Camel - only to be driven onto the Doom Bar.

... AND A HELPING SOUL

As you stand on the harbour wall at Padstow, look due east towards the rounded hill which forces the Camel to swing left and then right on its way from Wadebridge. This is Cant Hill. In the foreground is a charming piece of coastline bearing the name 'Gentle Jane'. You are right to ask: who was she? Gentle Jane belongs to legend, not to fact.

Somewhere around her Jane lived in peaceful seclusion. While some people thought her way of life lacked excitement or interest, she was happy enough, for she had lots of visitors. Especially on stormy nights she had many mouths to feed, many cuts and bruises to dress with the herbs she grew in her little garden. Animals came too: an exhausted fox, a starving dog, a wounded bird. All came to her; none was refused.

One day a gang of roving pirates, returning from a raid and assisting a wounded colleague, saw her light and hammered on her door, demanding food and shelter. But they had no need to display any aggression: opening the door immediately, Jane dressed the wounds of the injured pirate and provided food for them all. She never asked a question: to her even pirates were God's creatures in need of help as much as anyone else ... that was sufficient.

No-one knows when she died, or where she was buried. But this lovely stretch of the Camel still bears her name.

TREVONE

A BROTHERHOOD OF SHADOWS

The high, corrugated cliffs between Porthmissen and Gunver Head are home to a brotherhood of shadows, shadows of all colours and shades, busy little things working from dawn till dusk and always looking for opportunities to be helpful to some-one or something - they know full well that everything needs a shadow just as much as it needs sunlight. Each has his own ledge on these cliffs and each leaves long before the sun rises over Roughtor or Brown Willy to the east, returning only as it draws near the western horizon. Then the shadows sit on their ledges and tell each other what they have been doing during the day.

One summer's evening some time ago the shadows came home and rested on their ledges, gazing wistfully over the sea. Nothing broke the stillness except the low thunder of waves against the cliffs below. After a while they began to recount their day's experiences. A little dark shadow had been the first to leave that morning long before the sun had risen over Trevone. This one had gone to Crantock and found a poor, tired mother lying fast alseep with her baby beside her. Now though the baby was awake and becoming restless, so the shadow danced on the wall, helped by Brother Wind blowing gently through the window, which distracted little mite until her mother awoke. When the baby had been dressed the shadow followed her into the garden and now with the help of Brother Light made flickering patterns on the grass which kept her amused all day.

The next to speak was a crimson shadow. This one had been to St Columb Major where it had come across a young artist frustrated in his attempts to paint a rose bush in full bloom. So the shadow had gone into the heart of the roses and under the petals, creating exactly the crimson shadow that the artist had sought and was now able to capture on paper. A blue shadow had also helped an artist, a lady despairing of painting a large clump of sea holly. This shadow made its way along the sea holly's blue-veined leaves and cast a darker blue shadow over them, creating just the effect the lady had been seeking. Next, a black shadow had been caught up in the folds of a white cloud and on Denzel Downs had seen a field of barley which was ripening too quickly, sad because its heads were golden but its stalks still green. So this shadow had stretched itself over the field and kept the grain cool all day, helped occasionally by Brother Wind to make ripples along its surface. Another dark shadow had travelled as far as the Vale of Lanherne where it had heard an aged couple complaining of the debilitating effects of the unusually hot weather. It had climbed up the roof of their cottage, settled under the eaves when the swallows left and stretched itself across the front of the cottage, creating a shady patch where the couple could sit together all day. Next, a green shadow spoke of how it had seen a fish stranded in a small pool on Newquay sands and flashed its cool shade to prevent the pool becoming too hot for the fish.

Then up spoke one of the biggest of the shadows. It wanted to talk about its work on the most glorious day in the middle of May earlier in the year, when the headlands were glowing pink from the thrifts and the squills were flowing almost to the sea. Then it had been reluctant to leave the cliffs, just wanting to sit and enjoy the beauty and listen to the sky-larks' music, but the other shadows had reminded it of its responsibilities so it had slipped over the cliffs, jumped over the fields and run up the hills, flying with the clouds in the freshening wind, trailing its shadows over the cornfields and golden gorse until it had arrived at a large river winding between rounded hills, on one side of which were sand dunes and on the other a small town. There it settled near a large house where a young boy was looking out of the window over the garden. Because his legs were too weak to support him his only pleasure was to watch the light interplaying with shadows running races over the hills, but just now he was bored and sad. Help was needed. The big shadow asked the Keeper of the Winds to make Brother Wind stir itself so that the shadow could play with Brother Light, which they did all day over the yellow sands, over the fields of corn, over the river, over the flower-filled valley. As the sun travelled westwards and Brother Light followed, the shadow heard the boy tell his mother how he had had such a wonderful time watching the light and shadow playing giant's leapfrog, chasing each other as fast as the wind.

All the other shadows were so pleased at what the big shadow had done. Looking out from their ledges as the sun disappeared below the horizon, now they were silent, resting until the new dawn.

WALK DIRECTIONS

Distance	6½ miles (10.5km)	Time	3 hours
Map	OS Landranger 200 920754	Terrain	Though the walk begins in the town there are strenuous ascents and descents on the Coast Path, including one steep climb.

Car parking Park in the long-stay car park at the harbour

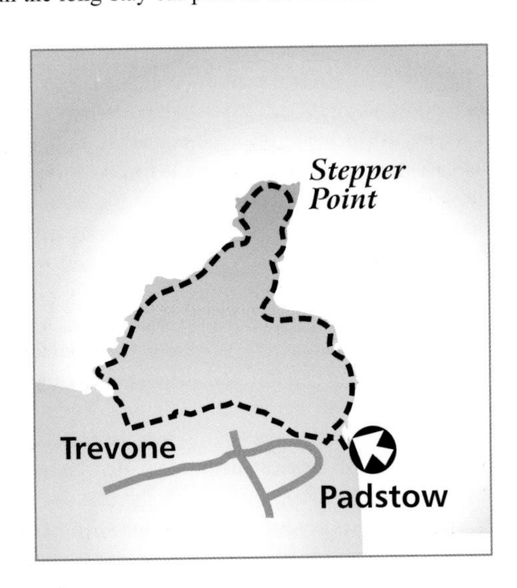

>> Walk to the harbour and turn left, keeping the shops on your left, and go down The Strand. At the Market Place turn left and then fork right into Lanadwell Street, keeping the cinema on your right. When you arrive at the public house which is the 'home of the 'Obby 'Oss', turn right and at the T-junction turn left into Church Street, now climbing gently and following the signs 'Bird Garden and Mansion'.

>> As you continue the climb, the church of St Petroc is on your left.
It was here that St Petroc founded a small monastery in AD 520, having sailed into the Camel estuary from Wales. There are many legends about him. When first landing he struck a rock and a spring flowed from it. Later he turned water into nectar. Later still he tamed a terrible dragon that was plundering the countryside, tying his stole round its neck and leading it down to the sea nearby from where it swam away and vanished over the horizon, never to be seen again!
Just past Tregirls Street turn right, passing Prideaux Place, and in about half a mile (.3km) go over the stile on your left signed 'Public Footpath'. Walk diagonally right across the field, over the stile, and then straight on to Trethillick Farm.

>> Go over another stile and on the road turn right. At the cross-roads turn left, signed 'Trevone'. Keep the field boundary on your left and go over the first stile on your left, following the path as you walk diagonally to your right. Go over two more stiles and when you come to the edge of the field go over yet another to join a track going downhill. Continue on this track as it meanders between farm buildings which soon becomes a path again leading diagonally left across a field to a gate.

>> At the gate go over the stile on its left between the hedges. Cross the footbridge and bear right, following the stream and at the stile bear diagonally left to climb the slope. Go over the stile at the top and head for the far gate, where you go through the kissing gate on its left.

>> You emerge onto a road where you turn right and walk downhill to Trevone and the beach.

>> Here you turn right to join the Coast Path, following the acorn signs up the cliffs, passing the spectacular round blow-hole and crossing the stile at the top. Continue on the Coast Path, but as you dip and rise do enjoy the cliff formations such as the double-arched 'Porthmissen Bridge', Langarrow Cove and Chimney Rock, a stack-like formation at Gunver Head. With Stepper Point ahead, you now walk along a more level section at the cliff-edge, passing Butter Cove and Pepper Cove (unusually named but perhaps related to shipwrecks or smuggling) before clmbing again to the daymark tower at Stepper Point.

Doom Bar is below to your right stretching across the estuary towards Daymer Bay. So appalling was the regular loss of life that various steps were taken to stem it. The forty-foot daymark was built by a group of merchants to enable ships negotiate Doom Bar as they entered the estuary. In addition they erected capstans on the point of the headland and at Trebetherick to winch ships in need of help and also removed vast amounts of rock to reduce the cross-winds which blew ships onto the Bar.

People say the sea grows darker as it approaches the Bar and the wind sighs mournfully, so it is worth standing very still to listen.

>> Continue along the Coast Path to the stile.

You can now see three or four miles up the River Camel and across to Pentire Point - and if the weather is clear as far as Bodmin Moor. Brea Hill and the crooked spire of St Enodoc church are prominent on the other side of the river.

>> Still following the acorn signs of the Coast Path, go through the kissing gate above Hawker's Cove and between the rows of former coastguards' and river pilots' cottages standing in line up the hill, to the slipway from where the Padstow lifeboat was launched for almost forty years from 1827 before the narrow channel was blocked by accumulating silt.

>> Cross the stile immediately in front and descend along the Coast Path as it sweeps round Tregirls sandy beach and to Harbour Cove. Still on the Coast Path, walk over the dunes before rejoining the path higher up and round St George's Cove.

Legend says that here in ancient times was a holy well, created when St George's horse struck a rock with its hoof and water gushed forth; there is no trace of it now.

>> Still on the Coast Path go over St Saviour's Point and then through the kissing gate to the War Memorial. From here you have a clear view of the comings and goings of ships and boats in the estuary, as far as Stepper Point on your left and Cant Hill to your right. Towards Padstow you can look down on another unusually named feature, Ship-my-Pumps Point, reminiscent of Padstow's maritime history.

>> The Path leads you into Padstow above North Quay. Walk round the quay to the harbour and your car.

PERRANZABULOE

A SAINT'S GIFT ...

St Piran must have overstayed his welcome in Ireland sometime during the sixth century for he annoyed King Angus of Munster to such an extent by his criticisms for taking a second wife that his neighbours there tied him to a millstone and threw him over a cliff into a stormy sea. That would have been the end for most of us ordinary mortals but as he hit the water the storm and the huge seas which had been raging died down, the sun came out and this millstone floated, carrying Piran calmly over the waves to the sandy beach here at Perranzabuloe. Amongst the spiky grass and prickly sea-holly on these bleak, windswept dunes, he built an oratory where his first followers were a badger, a bear and a fox.

St Piran gave his name to Perranzabuloe ('Piran in the sands') and went on to become the patron saint of tinners. Tradition tells us he actually discovered tin and is credited with exceptional knowledge of its processing. When he was building his fireplace he fitted a large black stone into the final space. Like all DIY enthusiasts, eager to try out his handiwork he lit a fire. As the flames became hot, then hotter, Piran noticed a stream of pure white metal trickling from that black stone. He had discovered the smelting of tin! Being the sort of person he was - and these saints were nothing if not pragmatic - he rushed outside and immediately passed on his discovery to every person he met. The local folk were overjoyed at their new-found prosperity and in return for the saint's generosity arranged a sumptuous celebratory feast. No doubt St Piran agreed to attend for it is said that he died drunk at the age of 206! The feast is still held annually. Moreover, wherever you see Cornishmen celebrating they are proud to display their standard - a flag with a white cross on a black background - St Piran's flag, representing white molten tin on a black rock base. In this way they keep his memory alive.

There are several tales of vanished cities or towns in Cornwall but a tale of a vanished oratory was actually confirmed in the nineteenth century. People living nearby spoke of a chapel dedicated to St Piran which had been lost under the sand dunes, and of travellers at night hearing the sound of bells chiming beneath their feet, guiding them to their destination. Then, after a violent storm in 1835 the tiny oratory re-emerged at Perranzabuloe. A shelter was built to protect it until that was destroyed by vandals and souvenir-hunters, so the oratory was re-buried in 1980.

But even in holy places, strange things can happen. One old lady had been scraping among the ruins of the church in the sands, and found a set of teeth which looked in good order. That night she had not been asleep long when she was disturbed by a voice calling, "*Give me my teeth. Give me my teeth.*" This frightened the old lady so much that she flung them out of the window, shouting to whoever or whatever was there to take them. As they fell onto the road she heard the sound of footsteps moving quickly away - and received no further demands for the teeth!

... AND A MERMAID'S REVENGE

In one of the deep valleys of Perranzabuloe, Pennaluna lived in a tied cottage with his wife, Honor, and their daughter, Selina. He was only a labourer employed by a wealthy yeoman who had several large farms in Perranzabuloe and elsewhere, but was hard-working, honest, able, and loyal, so after several years his employer promoted him to be manager of an outlying farm under the 'hind' or estate manager, Tom Chenalls. Like many of Pennaluna's neighbours, Chenalls was jealous of him, so was constantly looking for some reason to complain but every task was undertaken with care and speed.

Life for Pennaluna was not all a bed of roses. Though as industrious as her husband, Honor was a terrible snob. Worse still, Tom Chenalls had been brought up in the same village and had been rejected by her as a potential husband. Not surprisingly, this added to the hind's dislike of the family. There was a problem too with Selina. Now eighteeen years old and well-developed physically, she had not grown mentally to the same degree. As a child she had been plain but vigorous, energetic, curious and intelligent, but the village gossips went on about an occasion when Honor was bathing her daughter in a pool among the rocks at Perranporth - which was a known favourite of mermaids - the child had leapt from her mother's arms into the water and disappeared. When she re-appeared, swimming to the surface by herself, her face was brightly, beautifully different from before. Apparently Honor noticed nothing but all the aged crones declared her to be a changeling. Moreover, though admired by many of the young men around Perranzabuloe, she kept them all at a distance.

That was until the farm owner's nephew, Walter Trewoofe, came to Perranzabuloe to recover his health and strength after being away at war. As part of his treament, Walter took short walks on the shore. On one of these he saw Pennaluna and Selina wandering over the sands together. Struck by the girl's beauty, he took the earliest opportunity to speak to them, and later engineered further 'casual' meetings. His strength increased, and Selina was flattered by the attention of this refined young man, her father's own master.

Re-enter Tom Chenalls. Watching the young pair, the one attentive, the other receptive, he saw an opportunity to get at the Pennaluna parents. He knew Walter was easily led, so he talked about Selina, insinuating that her innocence was just a mask, assuring Walter she could be won with just a few words and then cast off - and the best way forward was through flattery of Honor Pennaluna. It worked. The mother could not see through the attention Walter showered on her daughter, and was openly proud that this was by some-one so much above their own class. Selina too was taken in, revelling in the whispers of love and passion, and too guileless to suspect anything other than straightforward, open honesty.

Now it was Walter's turn to take the initiative. He asked Tom Chenalls to find some way to send Pennaluna away for a while. This did not take long. Pennaluna was transferred to a neglected farm near Land's End to bring it into good condition again and it was three months before he managed to visit his home. Immediately he noticed a change in Selina. It was nothing he could put his finger on, just an ill-defined feeling that something was wrong. Another three months went by. Walter Trewoofe had left Perranzabuloe to live as before in London and Pennaluna returned home, his job done. But his daughter had become withdrawn and his wife was acting very secretively. Chenalls made the matter worse by constantly sneering at him, and when he made a remark about trying to ensnare the young man for a son-in-law Pennaluna lost his temper and hit him. Chenalls lost no time in reporting this indiscipline to the owner, embroidering it with an elaborate description of how the scheming Pennalunas had set out to catch young, innocent Walter. Pennaluna was dismissed.

Selina now took to staying in bed, eyes vacant, face unmoving, not eating, not talking, becoming weaker and weaker. Early one summer morning the sun shone through the small window of their humble cottage - onto a dead mother and a living baby. Selina was buried in the churchyard on the sands and the living went about their business. Tom Chenalls saw his life change though. From the day Selina died everything went wrong for him: crops failed, cattle died, hay-stacks caught fire, horses broke bones. He took to drink and was dismissed. Walter Trewoofe returned to Perranzabuloe and stood by him, getting him a small, lonely cottage on the cliffs. But he used his friend further as this out of the way place became the focus of drunken parties which Walter arranged and paid for.

One moonlit night Walter left the cottage and set out along the cliff-edge, zig-zagging through the furze and heather and then taking one of the paths which led to the seashore. He was sober enough to realise he had taken the wrong route and was cursing his own stupidity when he heard music. He stopped, listening intently. It was the soft, sweet voice of a woman singing sadly about betrayal by her lover. He followed the sound to a huge outcrop of rocks in the sands. Sitting in the mouth of a cavern was the most beautiful woman he had ever seen. She continued to sing, looking at the stars. It was several minutes before the woman noticed him. With a piercing shriek she turned to run into the cavern. Walter sprang forward and seized her by the arm.

She stood motionless, then slowly turned her head, her dark eyes beaming unnaturally. It was Selina's face. Walter loosened his hold. "*Go*!" she said. He could not move. "*Go, man*!" she repeated. He couldn't. Selina began to sing again, telling her former lover to go to the grave where she was sleeping, where she lay having been killed by her betrayer, and where he would experience the full extent of her grief. As Walter retraced his steps to the path from the sands he heard laughter, but could see no-one. In the morning he went to find Selina's grave. Here he sat on the sands, weeping inconsolably for a long time.

Walter Trewoofe changed. His health deteriorated. He became depressed. Local gossips said he had been 'ill-wished' and that Pennaluna and his wife were at the bottom of it. But Walter lived on, driven by the image of that beautiful face, which was and was not Selina's. Determined to resolve it, he returned to the cavern. This time there was no moon. Just as he reached the spot where the sands levelled off, compacted by the retreating tide, he heard the magical voice - now singing lightly, welcoming her lover. A low moaning wind blew along the shore-line as Walter listened, trembling with fear. The words were now reminding him that this was the anniversary of Selina Pennaluna's death. As Walter walked round the rocks a wild, echoing laugh cut through the air - and at the entrance to the cavern sat the same beautiful being. This time her face shone with happiness and she extended her arms towards him, welcoming him, encouraging him to sit and talk of their love. It was Selina's voice, it was Selina's face, but it was not Selina's body.

Speechless, he sat down. She wrapped her arms around his neck and drew him towards her as he recalled how often he had done this to her. She bent over him and he found himself looking into the eyes of the girl he had betrayed. She pressed her lips to his forehead. "*Kisses are as true at sea as they are false on land. You men kiss the earth-born maidens to betray them. Now you are mine till death.*" Death? He had dismissed the gossips' tales of Selina's mermaid origin as idle fantasy. Could they be true?

For hours Walter couldn't escape from the arms of this beautiful creature, every word of love torturing him. He noticed the tide rising rapidly. He heard the murmuring of the winds coming in from the sea. He saw the clouds massing into a storm. He begged her to let him go. He begged her foregiveness. He promised he would make up for his appalling, inexcusable behaviour. She again kissed his forehead. This time its coldness went through him. The waves rose around the rock on which they sat, reaching his waist. Still the mermaid would not let him go. The storm broke, lightning lit up the sands, thunder echoed along the cliffs. One crash shook the earth, and Tom Chenall's cottage burst into flames. Horrified, Walter saw Chenalls silhouetted on the ground, killed by a bolt of lightning.

At that moment a mountainous wave floated the pair off the rock. The mermaid held Walter by his hair, singing triumphantly. Along this coastline, in the roar of the storm thousands of voices were heard that night. The waves were full of creatures tossing the dying Walter from one to the other around the bay. Vengeance was wreaked by the innocent mermaid.

WALK DIRECTIONS

Distance	4 ½ miles	Time	2¼ hours
Map	OS Landranger 200 779545	Terrain	Moderate, some walking over beaches and gentle climbs on the Coast Path.

Car Parking Park your car at St Piran's Round, on the north side of B3285.

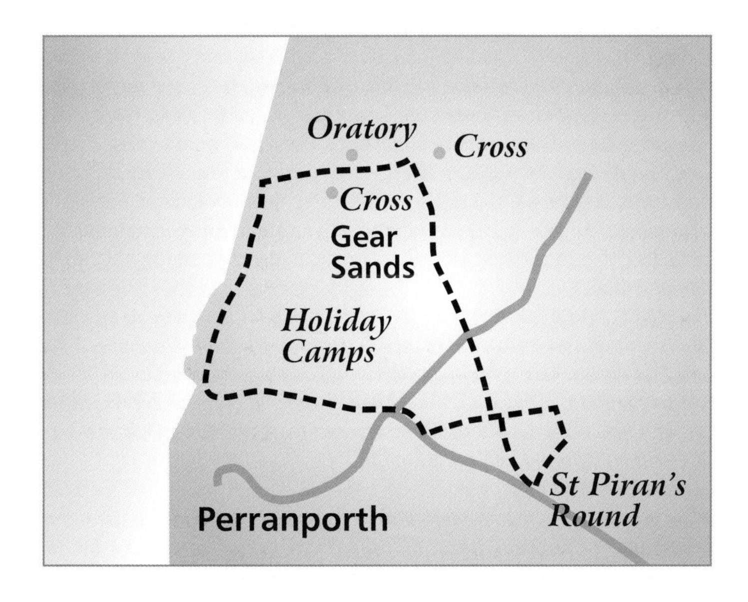

>> From the south-east corner of the Round, by the gate, take the track up left, past the white house.

The Round, which measures about 250 feet (45m) in diameter, was built as a hilltop fort during the late Iron Age, its earthen bank protecting the settlement inside. Later, it became a Plen-an-Gwary, a 'playing place' or theatre where the medieval Miracle Plays cycle were performed, possibly written between 1350 and 1500 at Glasney College, Penryn.

>> Turn left at the wider track and continue to the first house where you turn right as you see a sign to Hendravossan Farm. As you reach a row of cottages at Lower Rose take the public footpath into the hamlet of Rose.

>> Here, turn right and continue up the lane to the T-junction, going straight on by following the footpath sign through the gorse.

>> Before long you emerge onto Penhale Dunes, a Site of Special Scientific Interest, which has various species of unusual fauna and flora. Where the path divides, follow the yellow acorn waymark for the Coast Path, heading north towards the distant headland, Ligger Point, which marks the end of the two-mile stretch of Perran Sands.

>> Now bear to the right heading for the round-headed cross (not the traditional cross which is to your left).

This cross dates from c. AD 900. It is unusual in having three holes, and stands close to the church which was built in 1150 but later overcome by sand.

>> From the cross turn left, keeping the fence of the military area on your right. Soon you will see a sign indicating the route along the sandy track to St Piran's Oratory.

Though this is thought ot be one of the oldest churches in Cornwall, all you can see is a stone marking the site. The oratory is beneath your feet. It lay under the sand for a thousand years, before re-appearing a century and a half ago but has now been re-covered again.

>> Continue along the wider of the paths until you go over the sand dunes - and the great expanse of sea and sky opens before you.

Local legend says that Penhale Sands was once the site of Languna, a great city with seven churches. In some way the inhabitants must have invoked the wrath of God and in retribution the entire place was covered by sand, burying it forever. Like many legends it probably had a kernel of truth: a settlement overwhelmed by sand seems possible when we know what happened to *St Piran's Oratory.*

>> Turn left and walk along the seaward edge of the dunes above the beach, with the caravan site on your left. After about 500 yards take the concrete road from the caravans down to the beach. At the far side of a small parking area follow the Coast Path waymark.

Where the cliff falls away on to the beach, you can look down onto Perranporth, which with St Agnes nearby was the setting for Winston Graham's 'Poldark' novels about life in the mining areas of eighteenth-century Cornwall. Perranporth and surrounding areas were mined heavily during the nineteenth century for tin, copper, lead and even silver. There were at least six mine shafts here, one of which was worked before 1750, but which in 1836 were amalgamated as Perran Consolidated and employed 100 people. The mine Ross Poldark owned at the end of the eighteenth century could well have been based on one of this group. At the foot of the cliff are the caverns and shafts created by miners working this outcrop of the Great Perran Iron Lode. This Lode was very important, producing 200,000 tons of iron in just over thirty years and undermining the whole area from the northern end of the beach to beyond St Agnes.

>> At the end of the cliff, before the start of the beach, take the path across the top of the golf course, from which you emerge onto the B3285. Cross the road, turn right to a footpath sign on your left and go over a stone stile, keeping the clubhouse on your right.

>> Walk diagonally left across the field to a wooden stile in a wire fence and head to the stone stile in the wall, after which you turn right.

>> In the far right corner of this field the path emerges onto a lane through the centre of Rose. Go past the telephone kiosk and turn right onto the public footpath by the hedge to your left. Go through a field of gorse, then through a small gate into another field. Pass through the kissing gate and climb a few steps in the corner of the field onto the road.

>> Turn right and when you reach the corner go over the stile. Cross the field diagonally until you emerge onto a small road, go down the steps on your left and follow the sandy path until you join the road. Here turn right and immediately right again over a stile. Follow the river round to the two bridges and your car.

LADOCK

GETTING THE BETTER OF THE DEVIL

The people of Ladock were proud of their church. There came a time though when they couldn't get the bells repaired because a demon disguised as an enormous black bird perched on the tower, terrifyng the congregation and making the most appalling noises during services. This went on for some time so they must have been relieved when Revd Woods was appointed as Rector. He brought a reputation as a successful exorcist willing to confront any demons and malevolent spirits which plagued their daily lives, getting rid of them by thrashing them with his special ebony walking stick.

This demon though was beyond the Rector's reach. So, knowing that no demon can withstand the sight of innocent children, Revd Woods arranged for twelve babies to be brought to church. There and then he baptised them and held up each in turn. But this was no ordinary bird. It was a clever, cunning demon. It refused to look and hid behind one of the pinnacles. Until, that is, one of the children began to cry, and as babies do set off the other eleven. What a racket! The demon looked down from the tower to see what was happening only to find itself staring at twelve innocent, lustily bawling babies. No demon could stand this. Letting out an unearthly screech it flew from the tower - and never returned.

The local folk were also proud of their wrestling champion, Jacky Trevail. Jacky was rightly confident of his abilities. After one contest in which he won a magnificent prize he issued a challenge to any man - and went further, "*In fact I wouldn't mind a bout with the Devil himself.*" Tired and after the customary drink, as he was making his way home slowly and unsteadily across a nearby common he met a man dressed as a clergyman whom he did not recognise but who congratulated him on his recent victory and asked him for a contest, wagering five guineas to Jacky's prize. At the time Jacky thought nothing of it for many clergyman, including his own Rector, were keen followers of the sport. What did surprise Jacky was that this one insisted they fight at midnight, with the excuse that it would never do for his parishioners to see him wrestling in broad daylight. Still, Jacky agreed and they arranged to meet the following night. They were on the point of shaking hands when Jacky caught sight of a cloven hoof under the vicar's cassock. He made his way home in fear and trembling, convinced he had sold his soul to the Devil.

Next day, Jacky couldn't wait to tell the rector. Revd Woods advised him to keep the arrangement but make sure he had a piece of paper bearing mystical signs and words next to his heart. Jacky did, and at midnight he and his mysterious opponent started wrestling. From the outset the stranger got the best of Jacky, seizing hold of his waistband and rising up from the ground until he began to think his end had come. But Jacky was not a worthy champion for nothing and, using all his experience, skills and training, put up a spirited resistance. Then his waistcoat touched his opponent. Immediately this strange 'clergyman' fell to the ground, squirming and rolling in agony. He was indeed the Devil himself!

The Devil sprang to his feet, accusing Jacky of hiding some weapon and ordering him to take off his waistcoat. Jacky refused and they fought on. The Devil was thrown again and lay flat on his back, belching brimstone flames. Up he sprang more furious than ever, now appealing to Jack's sense of fair play. "*Tell Parson Woods to go home. I'm powerless while he's looking on. I can see his eyes gleaming at me behind that hedge and he is mumbling something to himself.*" This time Jacky picked up his opponent in a 'Cornish hug' and flattened him for the third time. Immediately the sky darkened, and in the dim light Jacky watched in horror as the beaten wrestler's feet turned into the claws of a huge bird, his clothes became a pair of wings and he was transformed into a grotesque dragon - presumably a transmutation of the one which had earlier disrupted work in the church tower. The terrifying creature flew off into the dark, leaving a path of flame and as it got to the blackest cloud it revolved in the air, emitting forked lightning and thunder bolts.

Jacky remained the champion wrestler for many years but was very careful which challenges he accepted.

WALK DIRECTIONS

Distance	6¼ miles (10.1km)	Time	3 hours
Map	OS Landranger 204 895511	Terrain	Mainly easy with two gentle climbs, a stretch of woodland and some roadwalking.

Car Parking Park with consideration outside the church

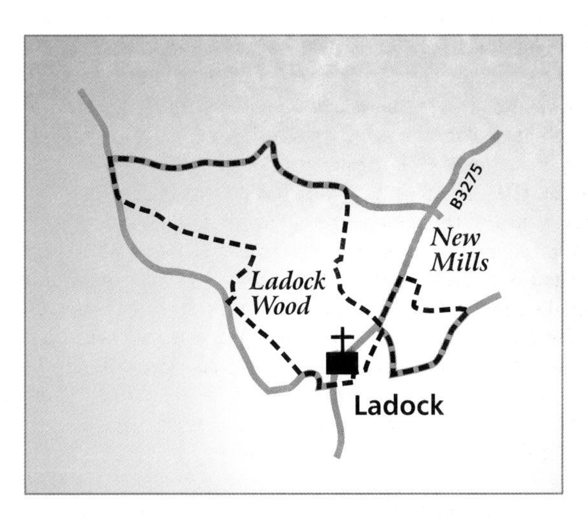

>> From the church walk to the main road (B3275), passing the inn on your left. At the junction turn left and then first right. This lane bends first to the right and then left, and just afterwards join the lane on your right signed 'Creens Farm'.

>> Go round the farm buildings on the public footpath and follow it as it bears diagonally left. Walk alongside the woodland, which is Ladock Wood, and in half a mile (.8km) at the first break into the wood turn right. Keep on this major track as you climb gently but steadily until its junction with another, but ignoring the footpath off to your left. At the junction turn left into St Enoder Wood. Follow this track through the woodland until you emerge onto a surfaced lane.

You are now in St Enoder parish, where Jacky Trevail saw the flaming thunderbolt strike the ground as the demon flew off.

>> Turn right and walk along this lane to reach the crossroads in about 400 yards (.4km). Turn right and walk along the road, passing houses on either side and then going through the northern stretch of St Enoder Wood, climbing gently all the while. Where the road bends to the left and then sharply right in a hairpin, the heavily wooded Trendeal Hill is to your left.

Not only are there devils and demons around here but piskeys as well. A nine-year-old boy disappeared from St Allen for over three weeks only to be found asleep on this hill on a bed of ferns. When woken he told a story of being taken by the Little People to a palace of silver and gold and being fed on fairy food.

>> Stay on the lane and go through the hamlet of Trendeal and where yiou leave the houses take the track on your right. This leads you towards Ladock Wood. Where this lane turns left, you go through the gate immediately in front following the public footpath sign. You enter a corner of Ladock Wood but soon emerge from the trees and first climb gently and then descend, equally gently, through a field, heading for a gate diagonally left. Go through onto the lane and at the junction with the road (again the B3275) turn left. Walk along the road and take the first lane on your right, signed 'Fentonladock'. This lane turns sharp right and when you get to the end go over the stile and turn left. Go through the field to the stile and then turn diagonally left to emerge over a stile onto a lane.

>> Turn right, passing houses on your left, and walk to the hamlet of Nankilly. Continue on this lane and take the first lane on your right. After about 300 yards (.51km) go over the signed stile on your left and follow the footpath through the fields, heading towards a gate immediately in front. Here join another lane which leads you to the church and your car.

MEVAGISSEY

JUST WHO RULES THE SEA?

Every-one in Mevagissey was connected with fishing. And every-one connected with fishing had heard of the Neptune of the Cornish Sea, Bucca Boo, and how he commanded his nine little men to row their longboat to a large pool near the cliffs around here to gather a rare plant called the Weed of Health. They also knew that whoever was fortunate to see this wonderful little boat, "*curved like a moon on her back*", and bring her into Mevagissey harbour would ensure good luck for himself and for the whole village.

Gradually over time this piece of folklore was forgotten, except by old fishermen like Merlin Legassick who in turn passed it on to his grandson, also named Merlin. Young Merlin was so entranced by the story that he searched every incoming tide for the little boat, especially as the fish had become scarce, the fisher-folk poor and most went about permanently hungry. But the fishing catch grew smaller and both the older and the younger Merlin longed for the little boat to come into Bucca Boo's Basin - if only they could get hold of it all their problems would be solved. But despite their wishing and watching the little boat did not come into the pool. Fishing almost stopped. Desperation was setting in.

One day young Merlin was sent to Polstreath beach to dig for bait with the usual instruction to keep a lookout for the little boat - the weather was pefect, the sea was calm and the mermen would have no difficulty getting into Mevagissey Bay. So urgently had this been impressed on him that instead he went to Bucca Boo's Basin where, though the tide was flowing fast, the sea was rougher than he had been led to expect. The waves were already breaking against the cliffs. The conditions were not right for the longboat. It wouldn't be long before all the people of Mevagissey died of hunger!

No sooner were such thoughts formulated than he heard a sound like some-one laughing - or was it a gull calling out, as they were always over these cliffs? The laughter was followed by a chorus of tiny voices singing - this was certainly not a gull but it might be, just might be Bucca Boo's little men coming into the Basin at last. Merlin climbed up the side of the rock and there in the pool was a little boat, no bigger than a toy and "*curved like the moon on her back*". It was full of tiny men, rowing straight towards where Merlin was crouching. This is what he had been looking out for. Here was his opportunity to save Mevagissey and the fishing. But how could he get hold of the boat? The little men were so intent on their rowing that they did not notice Merlin. Suddenly the one at the helm pointed to something glowing under the rim of the Basin. "*The Weed of Health,*" he called out. The others stopped and looked at the scarlet plant with its bright berries. But it was beyond their reach. They couldn't swim to it. They couldn't climb the rocks like the men of Mevagissey. They couldn't hope to take the Weed of Health back to their leader, Bucca Boo. Dismay turned to despair. Now was Merlin's chance. He let himself gently over the seaweed-covered side of the Basin but just as he was stretching out his hand one of the crew spotted him, gave a cry of alarm and the boat moved beyond his grasp. Undaunted, Merlin jumped into the sea to try to get hold of the boat.

When he came to the surface it had disappeared. He swam about the Basin searching under the seaweed and peering into the rocky holes, but to no avail. Now it was Merlin who was crestfallen. He couldn't go home and face his family after missing such an opportunity.

As he sat on the rim of the Basin he heard the laugh again, the same as before but now coming up from the pool - and there he saw the tiny boat on the exact spot from where it had disappeared! The helmsman and crew began to taunt Merlin and he had to accept that they had made him look foolish - but he was only trying to help the poor folks in Mevagissey. He told the little men the story his grandfather had told him and the reasons for his actions, and it was during this discussion that an idea began to emerge. Merlin might not be able to bring prosperity back to Mevagissey but he could get the little mermen the Weed of Health if they would tell him when the time was right to pick it - for it only blossoms and ripens two hours before the sun moves westwards.. The nine little men huddled together, whispering. Then the helmsman straightened up, saluted Merlin and declared solemnly, "*In the name of his Majesty, Bucca Boo of the Cornish Sea, we accept your kind offer to gather him the Weed of Health. In return we will make you an offer, subject to certain conditions, which will allow you to take us in our longboat into Mevagissey Harbour and so bring good luck to the fishing there.*" Merlin could hardly believe what he was hearing but the helmsman assured him of their good faith. The conditions, though, were to be strictly adhered to: the moment he has gathered the Weed of Health and dropped it into the pool he must leave; he must return to his village and stay there until they have rowed into the Quay, which will be just before the tide turns; he must not tell anyone, not even his parents or his grandfather, of them being in the Basin or of their promise to come into the harbour.

Merlin was confident he could adhere to the conditions. Flinging himself flat on the Basin's rim Merlin plucked as much Weed of Health as he could reach and dropped it into the pool. The little men stowed it away and Merlin set off back to Mevagissey. In the distance he could hear the little men singing, and as he ran up the streets he felt like singing, too. Just as the helmsman had warned it was indeed difficult for him not to tell every-one what he had seen and what was going to happen. It was worse when he got home as his grandfather questioned him about where he had been. It was best for him to get out of the house again so Merlin made for the top of the hill above the village. From here he could see the fishing boats returning and though they looked so picturesque it was obvious to him that this was yet another poor catch. The sun dropped behind the hill, its light reflected in the clouds towards Gorran Haven as he made his way down the hill and through the narrow, twisting steets. Everyone had gone to bed. It was the best place for miserable, starving people. But Merlin could not sleep and was soon out of the house again, racing to the quay - watched by an old pair of eyes from their cottage window.

In the distance a clock struck the hour. It was later than he had thought. The tide had already turned. Merlin had kept to the conditions - but would the little men keep to their promise? He heard a burst of laughter and, looking down, saw a longboat with her crew on the dark water. He ran down the stone steps and, encouraged by the nine little men, took hold of the little boat and brought her safely inside Mevagissey Quay until she lay beside his father's fishing boat. Now he would be able to tell people how he had won good luck for Mevagissey fishing.

Then he remembered what he and all the people of Mevagissey had suffered and as he turned away saw his grandfather walking towards him. Old Merlin had guessed what was afoot but by the time he arrived at the quay could see nothing except the fishing fleet riding the still water. It was then that he noticed something glowing softly on the horizon. Neither of them were ever sure what it was, but as young Merlin turned away from the open sea he thought he heard the little men singing in the distance.

All Mevagissey was in a ferment of excitement the next morning as young Merlin's story got about. Some believed it, some did not. Old Merlin merely replied that time would tell. And it did! From that night good times returned to the village, to its fishing folk, and more particularly to the Legassick household which became very prosperous. Though in other areas of Cornwall fishing catches remained meagre, in Mevagissey there was never again any need for anybody to go to bed on an empty stomach.

GORRAN

THE END OF A TROUBLESOME GIANT

A huge earthwork stretches from one cliff to another across the promontory in Gorran, in most places about twenty-four feet high and twenty feet across. No matter what archaeologists tell you about how ancient people laboured for years to make this defensive fortification, it was built by a giant, and moreover he did it in a single night! This giant lived on the promontory and from here terrorised the neighbourhood to such an extent that when a local doctor devised a strategy for getting rid of him, the locals were mightily relieved.

The giant was omnivorous - children were his preferred food - but one day he ate something which upset his digestive system. His groans and roars could be heard for miles, frightening the villagers even more. He sent a message to the doctor and he, braver than most, set off to visit the patient. By this time the giant was rolling about in pain, destroying everything around him, and the doctor - somewhat undoctorly - came to the conclusion that rather than treat the patient it was in every-one's best interests to get rid of the monster.

After a cursory examination the doctor made his recommendation, and took his opportunity: the giant must be bled, and to ensure relief from the painful symptoms he must fill a large hole in the cliff with his blood. It was unusual for this giant to be compliant but, urging the doctor to work as quickly as he could, he extended his arm across the hole and the blood began to gush. Certainly the treatment worked. The giant's pain decreased and he was happy to allow the stream to continue to flow into the hole. But weaker and weaker he became, more and more faint, until the doctor was able to kick him over the cliff edge to his death.

The promontory, Dodman - or Dead Man - Point, is called after the dead giant while the spot onto which he fell is known as 'The Giant's House'. As for the hole into which his blood flowed so freely, it has been noted ever since for its luxuriant growth of ivy.

WALK DIRECTIONS

Distance	11 miles (17.7km)	Time	5½ hours
Map	OS Landranger 204 013450	Terrain	Some road walking but mainly on the Coast Path which has a number of climbs and descents with a 374-foot assault on the Dodman.

Car Parking Park in the car park as you enter the village.

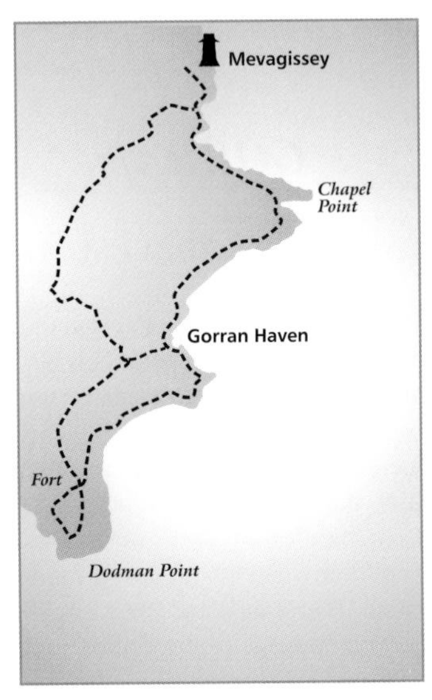

>> Walk through Mevagissey to the harbour, and when you reach the Ship Inn turn right and walk uphill with the harbour on your left.
Lil Baron was the landlady of this inn from 1910-47, and you may find yourself sitting next to her. If she vanishes, or your companions can't see her, just compare her ghost's likeness with a photo kept near the bar. There are other ghosts, too: of a young, weeping lady and of a bearded naval captain.
Still on this road pass the Harbour Lights pub but just where the road starts to descend, signed 'Portmellon', you turn right on the signed footpath and Penware Lane. Keep on this path as it becomes an unmade track and go between the hedges to emerge at a road signed 'Higher Well Park'.

>> Here you turn left and follow the road as it descends until you reach the sign for Penwarne Farm, where you turn right. Walk to the left of the farm buildings and follow the footpath sign through the gate, along the track and over a stile. Keep on this path as it curves along the side of the valley. Go through the gap in the hedge boundary ahead and keep walking in the same direction to another field boundary. Turn diagonally left and descend through the gorse to the footbridge in the bottom left corner of the field.

>> Go through the gate, past the house and at the road turn left. Go through the gate and over the footbridge. Now walk along the road as it ascends until you reach a gate on your right signed 'Bodrugan Wood Nature Reserve'. Take this sign and go

along the woodland path until keep to the right-hand fork. At the end of the wood go over the stile and along the path heading for the far right corner of the field, climbing to a stile in the fence.

>> Turn left and climb uphill to the stile. Now walk diagonally right to a stile and keep in this direction in the next field to the stile until you reach a lane. Turn left and keep on this lane before bearing right into the churchyard. Go round the church and down the steps onto the road.

>> Turn left, first going downhill and then uphill and bear left onto the road past the garage. On your right is a footpath sign so go over the stile, keeping to the left of the field. Go over the stile on your left and across the field before negotiating a stile which puts you onto a road.

>> Turn right and follow the road into Gorran Haven.

The fishing industry has a long history here. There is a record of it in 1270, when the powerful Bodrugans were the landowners. They remained here until the heir died in exile after supporting an unsuccessful rebellion against King Henry VII. The harbour was built in 1885, replacing an earlier one of 1585.

At the harbour turn right up Foxhole Lane and go up the steps to the footpath signed 'Vault Beach'. Go through the kissing gate and keep on the path as it goes down to a stile and another kissing gate which puts you onto the Coast Path. Now keep on the Coast Path, keeping left where the path divides and going down the steps before passing round Maenease Point or Pen-a-maen. In front of you is the granite mass of Dodman Point, but first you have a steep ascent and then more ups-and-downs before you get there.

'Dodman' is an unusual name and derives from the Cornish 'tomen', meaning 'bank' or 'dyke', which will make sense later as we walk next to massive Iron Age fortifications.

>> Continue along the Coast Path as it goes round Vault Beach. The path forks here so keep right following the Coast Path waymark. Follow this path through the kissing gate and over a stile into a small wood.

From here you can see the outer ramparts of the Iron Age cliff fort which covered this site.

Your path runs over the outer bank and when you reach a crossing of paths turn right and swing round in an arc.

On your left is the Bulwark, a massive bank stretching 700 yards (600m) across the neck of the promontory from the cliifs at Penveor Point on your left to those at High Point on your right. Allowing for erosion and alteration by farming over the intervening centuries, it is not hard to imagine that here was a formidable obstacle to anyone trying to attack the people inside. Don't forget though that it was built in one night by our giant!

>> Go over the stile and turn left around the bank. On your left is a path which leads inside the fort.

This, the largest cliff fort in Cornwall, covered over 40 acres (20 hectares), and was protected by the Bulwark and ditches from landward and cruel cliffs seaward. It contains burial mounds and an ancient strip field system.

Take the path through the fort and through the kissing gate before passing an eighteenth-century watch house with a pulpit-style lookout which in the nineteenth-century was used as an Admiralty signal station. Within a 100 yards (90m) you have reached Dodman Point, is marked by a giant granite cross erected in 1896 by a local vicar as a navigational aid to sailors.

>> At the cross continue to follow the Coast Path to turn sharp left at the next waymark and in about 400 yards (350m) cross the stile and turn right signed 'Penare'. You are now walking in the ditch of the Bulwarks.

Penare was the home of 'One-handed Carew' who lost a hand to a cannon ball at the seige of Ostend in 1601.

>> Keep to the main track ahead until you reach a metalled road, where you turn right. Continue uphill and at a junction with a road coming from your right go straight ahead onto the footpath signed 'Treveague'. Go through a gate and walk straight ahead, passing through two gates and following signs to 'Treveague'. At the third gate turn right, signed 'Gorran Haven'. Go past some houses on your left and Treveague Farm on your right until you come to a waymark post. Turn right into the farm buildings and then left behind the farmhouse itself. Go through the gate on your left and keep to the top of a steep field before descending to and crossing a small stream. This path puts you onto a surfaced lane where you turn left and then right at the junction with a main road, which leads into Gorran Haven.

>> Immediately in front of the cove turn left and walk uphill until you reach Cliff Road. Turn right and follow the Coast Path waymark through the houses. Walk uphill until you reach a footpath signed 'Portmellon' where you turn right. At the end of the lane go over the stile onto the Coast Path. Now keep following the waymarks for the Coast Path, going round Chapel Point onto a private surfaced drive. Turn right and at the main road turn right again downhill into Portmellon.

Sir Henry Bodrugan, a supporter of King Richard III, was chased to Turbot Point by Sir Richard Edgcumbe after Henry VII had gained the throne. Here Sir Henry rode his horse over the cliff and escaped to France in a waiting boat, and has been known ever since as 'Bodrugan's Leap'.

>> Turn right and stay on the road around the back of Portmellon beach then uphill again to join the Coast Path. The way to Mevagissey is well signed. Keep on the Coast Path until you pass Harbour Lights pub again. Now you descend into Mevagissey, going round the harbour and retracing your steps to your car.

LUXULYAN

THERE ARE HELPFUL PISKIES HERE, TOO.

On the Thursday before Christmas a group of tinners gathered at 'The Rising Sun' to hold their annual dinner to commemorate St Piran, the man who discovered tin. The party went well and when the time came for them to leave most had had too much to drink. One of them, John Sturtridge lived in Luxulyan itself so hadn't far to walk home. He had only got to Tregarden Downs when he bumped into a crowd of Small People enjoying a noisy games evening. They were amused by his un-coordinated, drunken state but he himself was more than a little frightened. Quickening his pace, he soon became disorienated on the Downs. His mood changed. He was annoyed at both himself and the Small Folk, when he heard a shout, "*Ho! and away to Par Beach*". Without thinking, John repeated the words and straight away found himself on Par sands. There the little people played for a while, then dancing round him cried out "*Ho! and away to Squire Tremayne's cellar*," which again John repeated. Within a blink of an eye he found himself with his little companions at Heligan. Here was as much beer and wine as John could ever have imagined and he certainly took opportunity to drown any fears he might still have. In fact he was so drunk that he was not able to repeat the next call: "*Oh! and away to Par Beach.*" The butler found him next morning stumbling befuddled amongst the barrels and bottles. Squire Tremayne didn't believe John's muddled and slurred explanation and he was jailed for burglary. Later, as theft was then a capital offence, he was sentenced to death.

The morning of his execution arrived. A large crowd gathered outside Bodmin Gaol. As John stood below the scaffold a little lady forced her way towards him. In a voice which John recognised she shrilled, "*Ho! and away to France.*" Without hesitating, John responded and was whisked away from under the noses of the Justices and officers. Both they and the crowd stood in silence, mouths agape in wonder - and disappointment.

WALK DIRECTIONS

Distance	4 miles (6.24km)	Time	2 hours
Map	OS Landranger 200 055583	Terrain	Easy, on footpaths and rural roads
Car Parking	Park at the King's Arms		

>> From the car park turn left and then right and walk across the bridges over the stream, water-meadows and railway. Now you begin to climb a hill and after about 100 yards (90m) turn right to go up the steps to the stile at the top. You emerge onto a road where you go straight ahead.

>> Before you reach the church turn right, passing the Luxulyan Institute and the Saints' Way waymark. At the post office turn right and at the former school go over the stile and cross the railway line again. At the far end of the bridge go through the gate and walk diagonally right across the fields. Cross two more stiles and at the third you emerge onto Joseph Treffry's Par Tramway. Bear slightly left and over the waymarked stile on the other side of the Tramway track.

The sides of Luxulyan valley are richly wooded, covered with mossy boulders, bracken and several species of fern. Some of the rocks are enormous. One, the Giant's Block, is the largest in Britain. Scattered among the boulders of ordinary granite are fine specimens of a pink porphyritic rock known as Luxulianite. The sarcophagus of the Duke of Wellington was hewn from a 70-ton specimen, and stands in St Paul's Cathedral.

>> Now turn left and walk alongside the Tramway to the end of the field. Cross the stile, go down the steps to the Saints' Way sign and turn right, walking between the hedges. Go over the viaduct and at the first lane on your left turn left down a steep hill. At the T-junction turn right and walk to Gatty's Bridge.

>> At the T-junction turn left, ascending gently into Luxulyan. At the church of St Sulien turn left and take the path until it forks. Keep right and when you join the road turn left, crossing the brdges to your car.

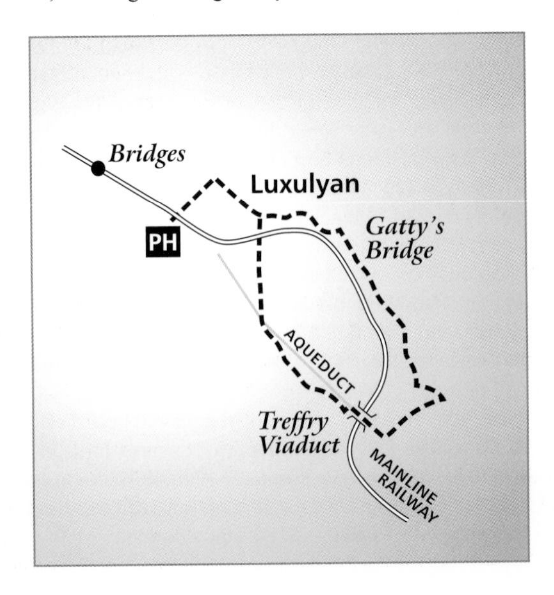

FOWEY

IN THE FOOTSTEPS OF TRISTAN AND ISEULT

When King Mark was ruler of Cornwall he had to swear allegiance to the Kingdom of Ireland, which required him to make a tribute to his fellow-king every third year of thirty men and thirty maidens, all aged fifteen. Tristan, Mark's nephew, was appalled.

Tristan had been brought up at King Mark's Court. His mother had died at his birth and his father, Melodias, King of Lyonesse, had spent many years in captivity, so Mark had taken him under his wing, treated him as his own son and given him a number of important duties, one of which was riding as the King's Champion. Tristan was also a knight of Arthur's Round Table dedicated to the code of chivalric honour, and vowed to end this traffic in slaves and concubines. He challenged the Irish champion, Marhault, the king's son, to single combat, the prize being the annulment of the agreement. In a fierce contest on St Sampson's Isle Tristan killed the Irish prince but was himself severely wounded by a poisoned sword. The only person who knew the antidote was the Irish queen but she was hardly likely to welcome her son's killer. So, desperately ill, Tristan concealed his real identity and travelled to Ireland where the queen and her daughter, Iseult the Fair, nursed him back to health.

On his return, Tristan spoke so often of Iseult's beauty and grace that King Mark, himself wifeless, considered the merits of an inter-dynastic marriage. Ambassadors were sent to Ireland, the match was agreed, and Tristan was despatched to bring the bride-to-be safely to Cornwall. As the wedding party were about to embark, Iseult's mother gave her daughter's maidservant, Brangwen, a magic potion, with instructions to ensure it was drunk by the royal couple, King Mark and Iseult, on their wedding night as it would bring them years of love and happiness. However, the maid was rather more careless than the queen had anticipated. She left the cup on a table where Tristan found it, had a drink and at the same time offered it to Iseult, suggesting she might like to taste the excellent wine. She did - and sealed their fate. Having shared the magic potion, they fell deeply, passionately, irretrievably in love.

True to his word, Tristan delivered Iseult the Fair to King Mark and the arranged marriage went ahead. To disguise the fact that she had lost her virginity to Tristan on the voyage they arranged for Brangwen to be the 'bride' in Mark's bed on the wedding night. Afterwards, however, Tristan and Iseult continued to meet in secret as frequently as they could. The king had no inkling of their liaison until the lovers were betrayed by the court dwarf, Frocin. Mark asked King Arthur for fair justice and Tristan was banished from Mark's court for ten years. This made future meetings difficult but Tristan thought of a scheme. At the rear of the king's palace was an orchard and a stream which flowed through Iseult's apartments. Tristan would throw a marked twig into the stream and when Iseult saw this simple signal she would go into the orchard to meet her lover. Eventually the barons at court discovered what was going on, told King Mark, and Tristan was again captured. Whilst imprisoned, he leapt to safety from the window of a chapel on a high cliff onto a sandy beach. Again using messages known only to themselves, the couple eloped, fleeing to the Forest of Morrois where they lived very happily - but only temporarily. Yet again they were discovered but still King Mark could not bear to kill the young man he had brought up as his own son. Again Tristan was banished.

Iseult's conscience though had been plaguing her and when she heard that her husband was sick with grief at her loss, she returned to him. To display her repentance she gave her silken robe to the church of St Samson, but Mark demanded she should swear on holy relics that she had never been unfaithful to him. This involved a journey to a reliquary across open countryside known as Blancheland, 'the White Land', but Iseult and the king's retinue set off, arriving eventually at a wide, deep stream, known as Le Mal Pas, or 'false step'. Here a leper leapt from the undergrowth, placed Iseult on his shoulders and waded across the ford, putting her down on the far side before running off. Iseult was then able to swear truthfully that only Mark and the leper had ever been between her thighs, for the 'leper' was really Tristan in disguise. He had saved his beloved from dishonour and probable death.

Only now accepting that he will never be able to be with the woman he loves, overcome by sadness and remorse, Tristan became a mercenary in Brittany where he met and married a local girl, Iseult of the White Hands. Though this Iseult was the daughter of the Duke of Brittany she was a substitute in name only for his real love. He could not put Iseult the Fair out of his thoughts and was unable to consummate his marriage. Probably to try to take his mind off this state of affairs, he continued as a mercenary and in one battle was severely wounded. Knowing only his Iseult could revive his failing health and longing to see her again before he died, Tristan sent for her, giving instructions to his messengers to hoist white sails on the ship if she was returning to Brittany with them and black sails if she was not. It is no surprise that his wife, Iseult of the White Hands, became jealous. As the ship approached she saw a white sail billowing in the breeze but told her husband that it was carrying only black: Iseult the Fair was not coming. At this news, the despairing Tristan gave up his hold on life. But his true love was on board. She landed only to learn that Tristan was dead. Seeing his lifeless body she too died of grief.

King Mark was able to forgive their adultery. He had both bodies brought back to Cornwall and buried in his palace at Lancien. A rose grew from Tristan's tomb which bent towards his lover's grave - and no matter how often it was pruned it always grew again the same way.

This is the legend, but what of the fact? Near Fowey the story assumes a definite air of reality. If we drive along the road from Fowey to Par we pass a rather majestic granite pillar, almost eight feet (2.7m) tall. On one side the stone bears a weathered Latin inscription *Drustanus Hic Iacit Cunomori Filius*, 'Here lies Drustan, the son of Cunomorus.' Documentary research has identified Drustan with Tristan and Cunomorus with King Mark, who ruled the Celtic kingdom of Dumnonia during the early part of the sixth century century. So both men existed and can be located in time and place.

In practice the inscription adds an extra dimension to the story. Does it mean that Tristan was the <u>son</u> of Mark and not his nephew? Was this changed when the story was written down in the twelfth century to mask an incestuous relationship? It becomes more intriguing. In the sixteenth century the antiquarian John Leland saw another line of inscription on the stone which, though now eroded away, could have referred to Iseult the Fair. So all three of the major participants may have been mentioned on it.

Modern excavations suggest that the Iron Age earthwork at Castle Dore, dating originally to the third or fourth centuries BC, was refortified and refurbished during the Dark Ages. The principal addition in about AD 500 was a large wooden hall, some 90 feet (27m) by 40 (13m) feet, surrounded by other buildings. There can be no doubt that this stronghold was important at the time and was the seat of Cunomorus/Mark - and the stone marking Drustan's/Tristan's grave was discovered here originally, before being moved to its present location. Local place-names too suggest that here was a chieftain's demesne: Castle Tregae (dwelling near the castle), Kilmarth (Mark's grove) and Garhules (the castle of Gorlois) - and Gorlois was the husband of Ygraine, who gave birth to the future King Arthur. This interesting slant to the story may offer some credibility to aspects of the Arthurian legend.

There is more to think about as we go on the walk. We are told that Mark and his queen worshipped at the church of St Samson. Only a short distance from Castle Dore, above the quiet, sheltered, tiny, waterside village of Golant, the parish church is dedicated to St Sampson. Then there is Mark's palace. Mark reigned from Lancien. A farm only a mile and a half north of Castle Dore is now called Lantyan, and there are records showing that as late as the fourteenth century it was the centre of a large manor whose lord held jurisdiction over lands spreading between St Germans and Lizard Point. Was this localised power the last vestige of the ancient Cornish kings? Does Lantyan Wood still keep its secret of the lovers, silent and watchful on the banks of the River Fowey? One final twist. The chapel from which Tristan leapt has been located at either Chapel Point near Mevagissey or St Catherine's Point near Fowey.

So where does this leave us? Tristan (Drustanus) and King Mark (Cunomorus) seem to have existed in the sixth century, conceivably at the same time as but certainly more convincingly than King Arthur. But the localities of the Tristan story are undeniable, as we shall soon find out.

WALK DIRECTIONS

Distance 4½ miles (7.25km) Time 2¼ hours
Map OS Landranger 200 121553 Terrain There are steep climbs on roads and tracks.
Car Parking Park in the layby at St Sampson's church.

>> Take the footpath, signed 'Saints' Way', opposite the layby. Continue with the hedge on your right until where it bends to the right you walk straight ahead and cross over the stile. Maintaining the same direction, go over the next stile onto the metalled road, signed 'Bellscat Farm' to the left. Cross the road, and the stile.
From this stile you can see the earthwork of Castle Dore on the hilltop.

>> You now descend towards the valley bottom, cross over the stile and head towards another stile at the gate. As you emerge onto the road turn left and follow this road

gently uphill. At the T-junction, turn right and continue on this road until you go through the first field-gate on your right. Now descend diagonally left heading towards the buildings of Lawhibbet Farm.

>> At the bottom of this descent go to the stile, passing to the left of the farmhouse and to the farm lane. Continue in this direction until you arrive at the road (B3269). Here, turn left and when you arrive at the signs for 'Castle Dore' turn left and up to the ancient fort.

You can walk round the site, which takes about 20 minutes, and climb to the top of the earth walls, where you can savour the splendid views it commands. In Mark's day the sea came up much nearer than now and the military advantages of its location are clear.

>> Retrace your steps to the road and at the first junction, at the hamlet of Castledore, turn left. You now descend for about half a mile to the crossroads, signed to your left 'YHA', where you turn right onto another surfaced road, passing the entrance to Torfrey Nurseries.

Penquite Youth Hostel must be one of the most splendid in the country, housed in a beautiful Italianate stucco mansion built in the 1840s by a Colonel Peard.

At the T-junction turn left until the road bends left, where you turn right into the field, taking the path between the hedges. Now you begin to descend steeply and cross the stream before ascending equally steeply up the other side of the valley. Head towards the derelict shed where you turn right and immediately left to emerge onto the metalled road.

>> Walk past two gates and follow the footpath sign on your left, before the buildings of Penventinue Farm. At the next gate, cross over the stile signed 'Saints' Way' and with the hedge on your left, walk downhill, continuing to descend through the woods. Cross the stream on the stepping stones at the head of Bodmin Pill and climb upwards, still following the path as it runs parallel to the River Fowey.

'Pill' seems a strange word to be using in this context but is Celtic and means a tidal creek. In medieval times this little inlet was used by quite large trading vessels owned by rich merchants from Bodmin and Lostwithiel which came in here to avoid paying harbour dues at Fowey. Plus ca change!

Where the path divides take the upper one. Cross the slate stile. Very soon you arrive in Golant.

>> Go straight across Fore Street, and continue up the steep hill, passing the Village Institute before turning right for St Sampson's church and your car.

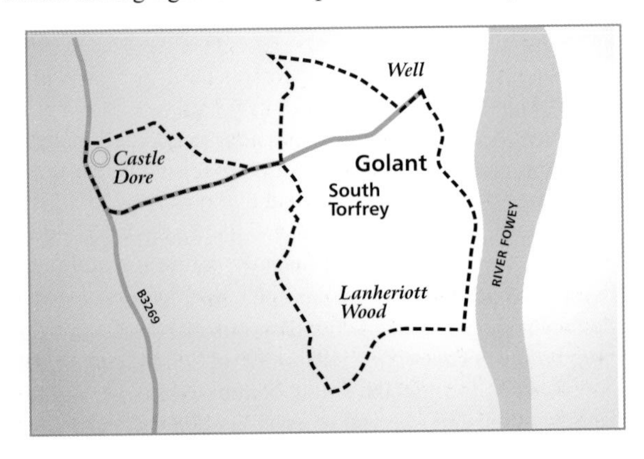

POLPERRO, TALLAND AND LOOE

OF DEVILS AND SPOOKY SMUGGLERS ...

Not so long ago the streets of Polperro rattled to the sound of pilchard barrels by day, brandy casks and tobacco bales by night. But some-thing else was at work. In the slate formations behind the village is a good example of what geologists call a fault, caused by movement in the earth's crust. Our forebears had another explanation. Here the mighty ruler of the realms of darkness created his own Devil's Doorway.

It is well known that the Devil is particularly fond of riding around in the dark to see how his disciples are getting on and if there are any more to enlist - and Polperro is where he came up from his subterranean territory. One night as he emerged in his flaming chariot, he burst through the slate rocks just here, leaving this huge rent. Exhilarated by the wind in its mane, his gigantic jet-black horse reared and pawed the air, striking sparks from the rock. Where its hoof struck the ground again with a force which shook the whole country, a deep impression of his burning foot was left behind. Still not convinced? Then go and look at the hoof-shaped pool, which is surely enough evidence for even the most sceptical of us.

You can see why Talland was a favourite spot for Polperro smugglers. It is a lonely place, offers good opportunities for unobserved landings and has a solitary church where kegs could be stored, waiting their secretive journey either inland in wagons over ancient tracks across Bodmin Moor or to Polperro hidden in carts taking seaweed for manure on the fields.

Do you know why the church was built in this spot? Originally, the parishioners planned it to be well inland at a place called Pulpit but each time the masons had left their day's work the stones were moved, mysteriously and inexplicably, to where the church now stands. Not surprisingly the builders got fed up with this, until one day a voice explained

Build my church on Talland Hill
And you will my wish fulfil.

So they did, and it has been here ever since.

And if that was not enough there was a time in the eighteenth century when Talland church had a reputation to make anyone shudder. Local folk, as they glanced over their shoulders, reported strange, moving, semi-luminous figures in the churchyard at night: clearly it was haunted by devils, wraiths and terrible apparitions. Thank goodness they had Richard Dodge as their vicar. He was an exorcist of the highest order, eager and willing to wrestle with even the most troublesome ghosts. But there were also those who whispered that he maintained a band of diabolic familiars which each night went to the vicarage to act as his servants. These, went the rumour, lurked in the churchyard and got even with humankind by pinching, smacking and playing tricks on anyone sufficiently daring - or rash - to pass this way. One exceptionally dark night one man even got a black eye! While under the influence of drink Zack Chowne met a crowd of friends and invited them to join him at the local inn - but called them by name and in return was struck with a sledge-hammer. So was the real truth that these mischievous 'fiends' were local smugglers in disguise, engaged in their profitable nightime business while taking opportunity to have fun with otherwise staid parishioners?

Nor did the Devil have his own way here. One night, the Revd Dodge heard from Abraham Mills, vicar of nearby Lanreath, of how some of the latter's parishioners had been terrified by a black coach driven by a ghost and pulled by headless horses. The following evening the two clergymen left Lanreath rectory on horseback and reached Blackadon Moor about eleven o'clock. The Moor is bleak and dismal during the day but now they could see nothing nor hear anything but the wind whistling across the bare hill. No matter how they searched in the darkness, no coach and driver appeared.

Agreeing to meet again, Revd Mills set off for his rectory and Parson Dodge rode across the moor towards Talland. His horse kept up a good pace, but as they approached the bottom of a deep valley it became uneasy, pricking its ears, snorting and moving from side to side as if something was in the way. The Parson urged it on but would not go forward. Dodge could see nothing. He whipped the horse and spurred it, dismounted and tried to drag it, but still it would not move. In desperation he remounted, threw the reins over its neck - and off the horse bolted in the direction they had come. Despite this uncomfortable ride they soon arrived at Blackadon.

As they approached Dodge saw, to his horror, the black coach with headless horses - and Revd Mills lying on the ground. He was just about to begin his prayers of exorcism when the coach-driver shouted, "*Dodge is come! I must begone*!", leapt into the coach and disappeared acoss the moor.

Apparently, the Revd Mills' own horse had taken fright at the apparition, thrown him and made for home as fast as it could. The sound of its hoofs as it galloped madly through Lanreath woke the villagers and a sizeable group set off towards Blackadon. There they discovered their rector, held up by Parson Dodge, but his speech was incoherent and he was in shock from some terrible fright. Fortunately, after a few days Revd Mills recovered. Parson Dodge got safely back to Talland. Since then nothing has been seen or heard of the black ghost or his coach and headless horses.

The more sceptical, though, thought that Parson Dodge was in league with local smugglers and made up his stories of exorcism and satanic apparitions in Bridle Lane, on the beach and on the Moor to scare off prying Excisemen. It worked.

... AND CUNNING SMUGGLERS

In the eighteenth century, Black Joan and her brother Fyn lived on Looe Island, where their major occupation was hiding smuggled goods in the tunnels they had dug in the rock. Before then they had lived with their father, an outlaw, on Mewstone rock. This was a time when Customs Officers were easily bribed, but as insurance Black Joan and her brother also had an arrangement with a farmer on the mainland who signalled to them by riding a white horse when Excisemen were about or by travelling on foot when the coast was clear.

So successful were Fyn and Black Joan that the Revenue men knew something like this must be happening, but couldn't catch them at it. So a guard was stationed on the Island to stop them running ashore the large stocks of contraband they had hidden away. The Officers had reckoned without Black Joan. One day, in great panic, she ran to the guard, weeping that her boat had slipped its moorings and was floating away on the tide. The guard leapt up: here was an opportunity to get on the right side of the locals and especially of this young woman. He soon secured Joan's boat - but didn't see a whole swarm of them on the other side of the Island, goods piled high and with every smuggler in Looe rowing furiously to the mainland. The 'free-trading' continued and Fyn and Joan were able to keep contraband brandy flowing freely. But the Revenue men never again trusted their guard on the Island.

Thank goodness Black Joan was never caught for this was a time when women were treated particularly harshly. In 1671 a woman from Looe was accused of a number of crimes: of hindering the English fleet in the war against the Dutch, of responsibility for the Queen's barrenness, and of causing a bull to kill a Colonel Robinson, the local MP, because he prosecuted non-conformists. Was she really so effective? Actually, the evidence against her was that a number of cats had been seen dancing in the air and that she had several marks on her body where the Devil had sucked her. She was found guilty of her crimes and sent to gaol, though mercifully the sentence was short.

WALK DIRECTIONS

Distance	10 Miles (11.6km)	Time	5¼ hours
Map	OS Landranger 201 205515	Terrain	The Coast Path is relatively level and undemanding, but there are three steep climbs (two uphill and one down) *en route.*

Car Parking Park in the Crumplehorn car park at Polperro

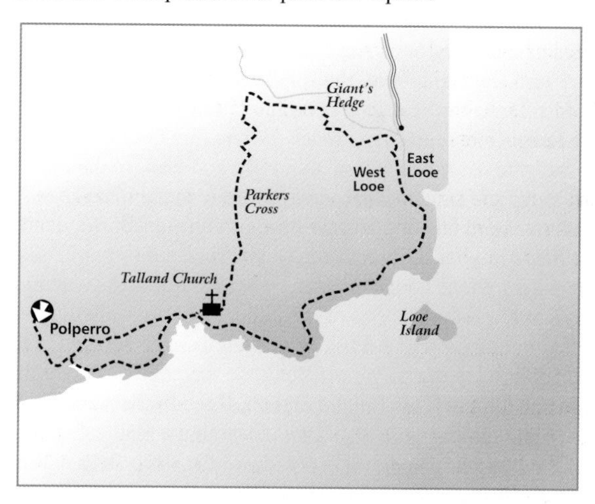

\>> Leave the car park with Crumplehorn Mill on your left, taking the road down into the main part of the village. As this road turns right at the bottom of the hill, continue straight ahead and follow the sign to the Harbour to your right. Go along the left side of the harbour, passing the Shell House and Heritage Museum. As you leave the harbour keep to the metalled path going uphill.

\>> Where this path forks at the sign 'The Warren', bear left, keeping on the metalled path until it becomes an unmade track between two hedges. Now you are on the Coast Path, heading towards Talland Bay.

>> Where the Path forks, bear right signed 'Talland' until you reach a stone cross. From here you can see Talland church and appreciate its significance for sailors and smugglers. Continue on the Coast Path until you join a tarmac driveway on your right. When this bears to the left, you turn right, still following the Coast Path signs. Go down the steps and then steeply downhill to Talland Bay.

>> At the bottom of the lane, bear left next to a cottage and follow the 'Coast Path' sign. Continue along this to Looe, going through National Trust property at Hendersick. The path changes direction opposite the jagged Hore Stone and Bridge Rocks, after which you can see Looe Island offshore. As you go across the field at Hannafore, continue into West Looe via the steps on your right and walk along the quayside. Go under the river bridge, past the shops, and into Millpool car park.

>> Cross through the car park and, keeping the West Looe River on your right, take the Woodland Walk towards the wooded slopes. Go past the Information Board towards the gate signed 'Watergate', but just before reaching it turn left, taking the path which climbs steeply through Kilminorth Woods, across the Giant's Hedge.

'One day the Devil, having nothing to do,
Built a great hedge from Lerryn to Looe.'

So says an old rhyme though tradition now ascribes it to a giant! This seven-mile earthwork stretches from the tidal head of the Lerryn River to West Looe and marked the northern boundary of a post-Roman kingdom, possibly of some-one who owed allegiance to King Mark.

>> When you reach a path junction, go straight across then immediately right to the broad track. Cross this and bear right, still ascending through the woods. Go through a gap in the bank and then turn left to walk alongside it to a wooden stile.

>> Go over and cross the field diagonally to the two gates at the top. Go through the right-hand gate into the next field and again head for the right-hand one of another pair. Here turn right following the waymark, walking downhill by keeping to the right hand side. At the next gate continue to follow the waymark, bearing left away from the hedge and alongside a fence. Where this field narrows into a track, go through the gate. At the next gate turn right and walk to the metalled lane.

>> Turn left along the lane as it ascends gradually to the main road (A387).

>> Cross this road and take the lane in front of you signed 'Waylands Farm'. Where this lane bears to your left, cross the waymarked stile straight ahead to a camping field. Here keep to the hedge on your right and follow the waymark. Climb the stile on your right almost at the end of this field, and now walk diagonally right across the field, aiming to where electricity cables cross the hedge. Go through the gate.

>> Bear right following the waymark along the top edge of the field. From here you can again see the tower of Talland church. Keep to the right hand boundary, and to the right of the Landmark, one of two measuring a nautical mile for ships on speed trials. At the bottom, go over the stile, down the steep steps and onto the metalled lane. Turn right and walk to the church. Keep going downhill to the beach.

>> From Talland beach turn left along the road in front of the house and take the Coast Path uphill. Where this Path bears to your left (you are now retracing your earlier route) continue straight ahead on the metalled lane, ascending steeply. Go past the drive of a house on your left, still climbing, and where the road levels off and joins another road, go straight ahead, past the houses and school.

>> At the T-junction bear left, now going downhill steeply, to Polperro. Keep to your right and retrace your earlier route through the village to your car.

COTEHELE

HOW THE CHAPEL CAME TO BE BUILT ...

Though dating originally from 1353, the present Cotehele was built about 1550 with both privacy and defence in mind. Before moving to Mount Edgcumbe in the seventeenth century, the Edgcumbes lived here and certainly left their mark. In the grounds by the river you will find a small chapel - and therein lies a tale.

In all the squabbles surrounding the Wars of the Roses and its after-effects, Richard Edgcumbe had been a constant supporter of Henry, the Lancastrian Earl of Richmond. Even so, the great Cornish families were as divided then as they were in the Civil War a century and a half later, and took this, like every other opportunity, to settle old quarrels, rivalries and jealousies - sometimes amounting to feuds.

In 1484, when Richard III had been on the throne for just over a year and was determined to eliminate as many of his former enemies as possible, Richard Edgcumbe was being hunted by the king's soldiers led by another Cornishman, Sir Henry Trenowth, also known as Henry de Bodrugan, a supporter of the House of York, a former freebooter who had been made Sheriff of the county by King Edward IV, and who had been rewarded by the new King Richard with the manors of Trelawne and Tywardreath. After many years travelling in England offering support to what he hoped would be the winning side, Richard Edgcumbe returned home to Cotehele, fully aware that he was a marked man. All his own soldiers and workers on the estate were put on the alert. And the moment he had dreaded arrived - soldiers were seen approaching Cotehele. Richard fled into the woods. The pursuers were determined and stuck doggedly to his trail. Slowly they were catching up with him. Then he was faced with real danger: Richard reached an overhanging rock high above the river and realised his path was blocked. With nothing to lose, he threw his hat and a large stone into the flowing waters, clung precariously beneath the overhang and remained absolutely still. The cunning plan worked. His pursuers heard the splash and seeing the hat in the swirling river Trenowth assumed Richard had tried to get across somehow, had slipped and drowned. Trenowth abandoned his search and his soldiers returned to their base. Richard clambered up the cliff and stole back into the house, knowing that he would have to leave the country. From Cotehele he escaped to France, returning just before the battle of Bosworth. For his unwavering support and valour he was knighted on the battlefield by the new king, Henry Tudor. The first thing he did when he got back home was to build a chapel on the very spot where he had been saved.

Yet there is a tide in the affairs of men ... The tables were turned. In 1487 Sir Henry Trenowth de Bodrugan was now the outlaw and Sir Richard, armed with an arrest warrant, pursued him to his home on the cliffs of Chapel Point near Mevagissey. Surrounded by his Lancastrian enemies Trenowth jumped from a spot still known as 'Bodrugan's Leap' into a boat bound for France. When the boat was far enough from shore he cursed the descendants of his would-be captors, Trevanion and Edgcumbe. If you follow the fortunes of the families from then on, you may think the curse worked.

... ONE LADY EDGCUMBE RISES AGAIN ...

Some two hundred years later, another of the Edgcumbes had an even stranger experience. By now the family had left Cotehele and were living in their new mansion at Mount Edgcumbe. In 1675, the mistress of the house, Lady Anne Montague, still a young woman, became very ill and lapsed into a coma. The doctors were called and after a while pronounced her dead. Three days later the grieving family arranged a lavish ceremony as her body was placed in the family vault beneath the chapel at Cotehele, and left her at peace with her ancestors.

But the sexton had other ideas. He had noticed that the body was buried with all its jewellery and finery. That same night, intent on helping himself, he went down into the vault and held up his lantern. The first thing he saw was a gold ring on her finger, and he began to tug it off. This was not as easy as he had thought, and he had to press and pinch the finger with one hand while holding it with the other - and her Ladyship's body stirred. The corpse moved further and focused its eyes on him. In abject terror the sexton dropped his light, his tools and his keys and bolted for his life, screaming for mercy.

Lady Edgcumbe got out of her coffin, took the lantern the sexton had dropped, made her way up the steps through the door he had thrown open and tottered unsteadily to the mansion. Her family were amazed but delighted to see her - but what we don't know is how they thanked the sexton.

Some five years later, in 1680, she had a son, Richard, who was later to become the first Baron Edgcumbe.

... AND ANOTHER HAS AN UNUSUAL PET

It was the wife of this Sir Richard who became so bored with the company she had to keep in the social life of this part of Cornwall that she took a pig as a companion, naming it Cupid. She became devoted to it and it in turn followed her everywhere, even accompanying her on visits to London, as it lived out his days in considerable comfort. On Cupid's death the Countess was distraught - and very soon afterwards a thirty-foot tall obelisk appeared on the estate. Was this erected in loving memory of Cupid? No-one knows, as there was no epitaph, though a report in a local newspaper claimed that it was and that Cupid had been buried in a gold casket underneath on the instruction of the Countess.

As you would expect there was much gossip about the bizarre relationship, accentuated by the satirist Dr John Wolcot under his pseudonym Peter Pindar in an ode entitled

Ode to the Countess of Mount Edgcumbe
On the Death of her Pet Pig Cupid
Oh! dry those tears so round and big,
Nor waste in sighs your precious wind,
Death only takes a little pig.
Your Lord and son are left behind!

In the 1860s the obelisk was moved to a hill near Cremyll, outside the Mount Edgcumbe estate. Was this to give it greater prominence or to get at the gold casket?

WALK DIRECTIONS

Distance 2 miles Time 1 hour
Map OS Landranger 201 424682 Terrain Most of this walk is through Danescombe Valley along excellent woodland tracks.
Car Parking Park at the main car park at Cotehele Quay.

>> From beside the entrance of the car park and just beyond the Cotehele Quay Gallery take the woodland path signed 'Danescombe' and go through the woods, gradually ascending to the Chapel.
Take time to look at the chapel. It is the one built about 1490 by Sir Richard Edgcumbe after his return from exile. A plaque inside gives details of Richard Edgcumbe's escape from Sir Henry Trenowth of Bodrugan.

>> Take the lower path away from the Chapel and continue on the woodland track, as it bears sharp right to the Viewpoint.
The viewpoint on your right is the spot where Richard Edgcumbe flung his cap into the waters below.
From here keep to the same path now descending through the woods.

>> When you arrive at a T-junction, bear left and go past the ruins of Danescombe Mill. You now begin to climb gradually following the course of a stream and passing two cottages. Follow the track over the stream and very shortly cross the stream going left over a wooden footbridge next to the converted engine house of Cotehele Consols Mine. Take the footpath to your right, going near to the stream and around a small pond.

>> Go through the woods and where the path forks at the bottom of the steps bear left, now walking uphill through the woods. Keep climbing, ignoring all the side paths, until you join a broad woodland track which takes you through an area of coniferous woodland to another fork.

>> Here bear right signed 'Cotehele House'. Pass above the dovecote then when you arrive at a T-junction turn left. Go through a gate and turn right, passing the entrance to Cotehele House.
This is where Richard Edgcumbe was living when he fled from Sir Henry Trenowth's men. It has survived as one of the finest Tudor buildings in England and gives insight into how the wealthier people lived in Tudor Cornwall.

>> Follow the road from the House and branch left, going downhill to Cotehele Quay and your car.

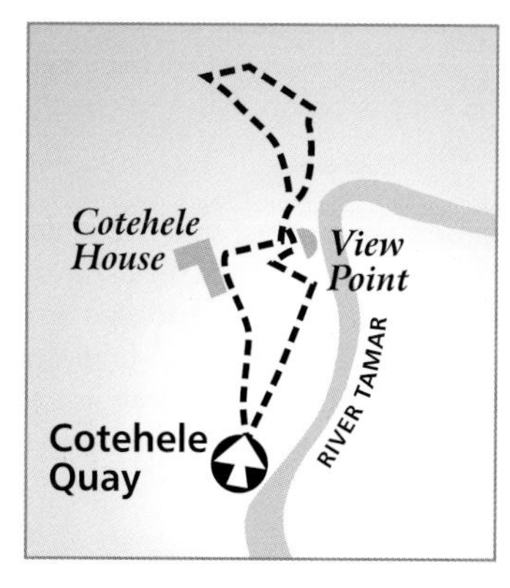

ANTONY

THE OLD WOMAN AND THE TOAD

An old woman called Alsey lived a cottage in Antony, one of a terrace owned by a shop-owner from Dock, as Devonport was then called. She was well-known for her violent temper and black moods, and it was for these rather than supernatural skills that she had earned the reputation of being a witch.

She had let her rent fall into considerable arrears and was terribly abusive to her landlord whenever he asked for it. Not surprisingly, even his patience ran out. He crossed the Tamar and walked to Antony determined to get his money and to turn the old termagant out of the cottage. They had an alarming row, in which the vociferous, vicious old woman sat in the doorway, cursing the landlord, his wife, "*the child she was carrying*" and everything belonging to him with such spite that the poor fellow was driven away, unpaid.

Even by the time he arrived back home he had not got over the ordeal, and was just telling his wife and young daughter what had happened when a customer came into the shop. His wife attended to the lady and was weighing out the orders when something fell from the rafters, knocking the scales out of her hand. Both women screamed.

The man and his daughter rushed into the shop and there on the counter saw an enormous, fat toad sprawling amongst the weights and scales. Almost without thinking, he dashed back into the living room, grabbed a pair of tongs and, grasping the toad, flung it behind a block of wood burning in the grate. Overcome with fright, his wife, who was in the later stages of pregnancy, fainted. The doctor was sent for and he ordered his patient to bed, instructing the husband to prepare for a premature delivery.

Such was the high level of anxiety and the attention the shopkeeper was paying to his wife that for an hour or two he forgot completely the cause of all this trouble, and certainly didn't go to see what had happened to the toad. Suddenly though, he heard from the room below the terrified cry of his daughter: "*Father, the toad, the toad*!" He rushed downstairs to find that the toad, though severely burned, was alive. It had crawled painfully over the blazing log, fallen amongst the ashes and was now struggling to escape by climbing over the fender, where at that moment it sat spitting. Again he snatched up the tongs - but at that precise moment a man from Antony ran into the shop to report that Alsey had fallen into the fire, possibly in a fit, and was nearly burned to death.

Shuddering, the shopkeeper threw the toad out into one of the flowerbeds before hurrying to Antony with the doctor. The house was gutted and the old woman so severely burned that they did not expect her to survive. Despite what she had said and done, the shopkeeper ensured Alsey received every possible attention. However, she never recovered consciousness and died during that night. Next morning, the toad lay dead just where it had landed with a splat. To his horror, as he picked it up the shopkeeper found it had exactly the same burns as those sustained by the old woman.

And their unborn child? A son arrived, and like many others from Dock became an officer in the navy. Unfortunately, later in his career his ship sank and he was drowned, leaving a grieving widow with an unborn child. Whether or not this was the consequence of the old woman's curse only those more skilled in witchcraft will be able to say.

WALK DIRECTIONS

Distance	9½ miles (12.1km)	Time	4 hours
Map	OS Landranger 201 398546	Terrain	Mainly level and easy on footpaths and Coast Path but with one steep climb and descent on a road.

Car Parking Park outside the church

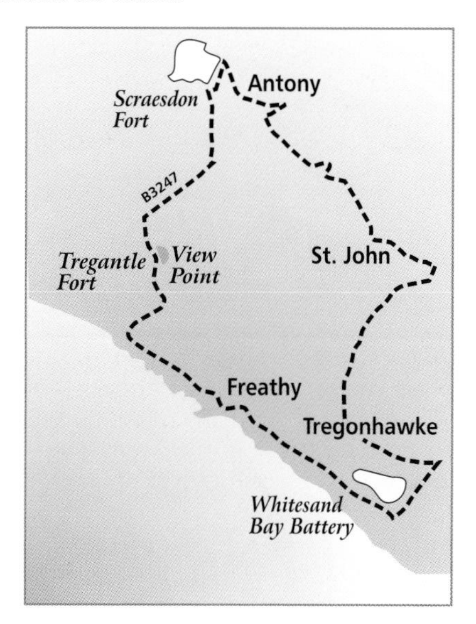

>> From the church turn right and walk along the road (B3247) into the village.
It was in one of these terraces of cottages that Alsey lived and where she had acquired the reputation of being a witch.
At the junction with the main road (A374) cross over and turn left.
You are now walking along the route which the shopkeeper from Dock/Devonport took whenever he came to his property in Antony. The only way for him was by ferry across the River Tamar, his most likely point being where the modern ferry crosses the Hamoaze at Torpoint.

>> Keep on this road for 600 yards (.4km), keeping the woodland on your right. At the end of this woodland take the signed path on your left to 'Scraesdon Fort'. Keep the fort on your right and at the surfaced lane turn right. After 100 yards (90m) take the footpath on your left which leads to the road (B3247). Turn right and walk along the road, passing a junction signed 'Lower Tregantle' on your left, and within a few yards take the footpath on your left.

>> This puts you onto a road which at this point serves also as part of the South West Coast Path. Turn left and then right following the Coast Path, passing over Freathy

Cliff and with Chamber Rock on your right. At Whitesand Bay Battery turn left onto the lane signed 'Tregonhawke' and walk to the hamlet.

>> Here turn left and walk with Millbrook Reservoir - and its splendid fishing - on your right. At the fork bear right along Withnoe Lane. Go straight over the crossroads and into the hamlet of Mendennick, having climbed steadily up Mendennick Hill.

>> At the cross roads turn left, signed 'St John', and follow the road into the village. Cross the bridge and turn left following signs to 'Antony'.

>> Keep the houses on your right and then the woodland on your right until you see the entrance to Wolsdon House on your left. Go up the drive and where you come to a copse turn right along the footpath. At the gate you emerge onto the road and turn left. At the next fork bear left, go over the crossroads with the school on your left, and take the footpath, signed 'Church', on your right.

>> This takes you to the church of St James and your car.

ST GERMANS

DANDO AND HIS DOGS

When you walk through St Germans your first impression is of a sleepy village of picturesque cottages and flower-filled gardens. It was not always so. In Anglo-Saxon times the church of St Germanus was Cornwall's busy cathedral and seat of the Cornish bishopric established by King Athelstan c. AD 936. It remained an important religious centre until 1050 when it was incorporated into a new diocese centred on Exeter. The church's great west door displays its importance, a masterpiece of Norman architecture and carving unrivalled in Cornwall, attracting visitors from all over the world. But go inside.

Here you will find some interesting pieces of wood. For years one oblong piece, carved on the face at one end and with a pivot at the other, lay in the belfry. Then a chair was discovered which had been built into the chancel wall, but devoid of a seat. When the two were put together the carved wood fitted exactly, and turned on its pivot, making up either a penitential sedile or a misericord - a choir seat, usually with a grotesque or humorous carving, with a small ledge which when the seat is tipped up forms a projection against which a monk could rest when standing. It is the only survivor of the cathedral choir seating. And the carving? The imagery is of a hunter, game slung over his shoulder on the stock of his cross-bow, with his hounds around his feet - but why?

Long ago Dando was a monk of St Germans Priory though he was not the usual sort of person one would expect to find. Clearly, his religious duties were low in his priorities and had been superseded by three major interests in his life: hunting, at which he spent most of his time with his hounds in the woodlands surrounding the monastery, drinking, and profanity with which he littered his conversations.

One hot Sunday in July he had spent the day hunting with a group of like-minded people around Erth Barton on the other side of the St Germans river. His hounds had bagged several deer and as the day was coming to an end he called to his companions to get him a drink, even if they had to go to hell for it because today was the Sabbath. A hunter not known to Dando came forward and offered a silver flask that was chained to his arm. Without even looking at the hooded figure Dando drank deeply. He was not, though, amused when turning round he noticed that the strange hunter had taken several head of his own game and launched into an argument, swearing profanely. That got him nowhere and in the end Dando declared that he'd go to hell to get them back. "*So you shall*," came the reply. The hunter lifted Dando off the ground, put him on to his own coal-black horse, and got up behind. In sight of everyone, the horse and its riders galloped away down Erth Hill, the hounds following close behind. When it reached the banks of the River Lynher the horse leapt far out into the waters at the spot known ever since as Dandypool. The waters boiled for a moment before closing over the horse, riders and hounds. That was the last ever seen of Dando. But even now the soul of the wild, lawless huntsman haunts the place and his baying hounds can be heard in the darkest hours of the night.

Why Dando? The name could be a corruption of Dawnay or Dandy, the knightly Lords of Cheviock in the Middle Ages.

WALK DIRECTIONS

Distance	3¼ miles (5.3km)	Time	2 hours
Map	OS Landranger 201 350575	Terrain	Mainly easy along footpaths and wide tracks through woodland, but with one gentle ascent/descent.

Car Parking Park at the railway station (well signed)

>> From the railway station walk to the road (B3249) and turn left. Continue on this road until you reach the church of St Germanus on your right.
We suggest you look at the great west door before going into the church. It is a magnificent example of Norman carving and indicates the church's importance as the seat of the Bishopric of Cornwall until 1050. It then became the church of an Augustinian Priory and was completed by the Canons in 1261 before they turned their attention to building for their own use and accommodation on the north side of the cloister garth. Inside the church, in the south nave, is the carved misericord portraying Dando and his dogs.

>> Outside the church is the imposing gateway to Port Eliot.
In 1539 the Priory was closed by King Henry VIII and the Canons departed. In 1540 the king's agents, having stripped it of everything of value, sold it as a private residence and eventually in 1564 it was bought by John Eliot, a gentleman of St Germans, for £500. Thus began the association which continues to this day. John Eliot had watched the Priory falling into ruin and used the stone to build his own house which from 1573 was known as Port-Elyot. The buildings were re-modelled in the eighteenth century.
To the left of the gateway is a signed footpath, which you should take through the woodland. Very soon you arrive at a fork of two larger tracks where you branch to the right. When you reach the houses turn right and walk alongside their gardens until you emerge from the woodland into a field. Keep going upwards in the same northerly direction into the hamlet of Lithiack, passing the lakes on your left.

>> At the first house turn left, keeping the lakes on your left, and in about 200 yards (175m) take the public footpath on your right, signed 'Keeper's Plantation'. Follow this track until you arrive at Penimble Plantation on your right. In a further 300 yards (270m) walk up the drive on your right to Penimble House. Just before the House turn right through the gate onto the track into Craggs Wood.
The woods were well-known to Dando, and amongst his favourite hunting places.
Keep on this track as it descends to the River Tiddy. Here turn right and walk alongside the river.

>> In about half a mile (.8km) you go through a gate into the grounds of the former Augustinian Priory where you take the first track to the left and walk alongside the river on your left.
Dando was a monk at the Priory and you are now walking alongside the pool in the River Lynher where he was last seen.

>> Where the track forks take the right hand branch and you will leave the Priory grounds by a gate onto a metalled lane. Walk down this lane to its junction with the road (B3249). Turn left and retrace your steps to the railway station and your car.

... AND BACK TO THE TAMAR

Apparently the Devil arrived at the Tamar and stood wondering whether to cross over into Cornwall, where he had never been before. "*No, I won't risk it,*" he said. "*Over there everyone's made into a saint and everything into a squab pie.*"

BIBLIOGRAPHY

Addicoat, Ian, and Buswell, Geoff (2003) *Mysteries of the Cornish Coast* Tiverton: Halsgrove

Bottrell, William (1880) *Traditions and Hearthside Stories of West Cornwall* Llanerch Press

Caine, Margaret, and Gorton, Alan (2001) *Curiosities of Cornwall* Seaforth: SB Publications

Courtney, M A (1973) *Cornish Feasts and Folklore* Wakefield: EP Publications

Garnett, William (1989) *Horrors and Hauntings in Cornwall* Padstow: Tabb House

Grigson, Geoffrey (1954) *Freedom Of The Parish* London: Phoenix

Hunt, Robert (1865) *Popular Romances of the West of England*

Hunt, Robert (1881) *Romances and Superstitions of the West of England*

Hunt, Robert (1993) *Ghosts, Demons and Spectres in Cornish Folklore* Redruth: Tor Mark

James, Beryl (1993) *Tales of the Saints' Way* Redruth: Dyllansow Truran

Jenner, Michael (1993) *Travellers' Companion to the West Country* London: Joseph

Jones, Sally (1980) *Legends of Cornwall* St Teath: Bossiney Books

Lacey, Robert (2003) *Great Tales from English History* London: Little, Brown

Stanier, Peter (1988) *The Work Of Giants* St Ives: St Ives Printing and Publishing Co.

Tregarthen, Enys (1940) *Piskey Folk* New York: John Day

Tor Mark Press (1997) *Strange Tales of the Cornish Coast*

Turner, J (1973) *Ghosts of the South West* Newton Abbot: David and Charles

Weatherill, Craig, and Devereux, Paul (2001) *Myths and Legends of Cornwall* *Wilmslow: Sigma*

White, Paul (1994) *Classic Cornish Anecdotes* Redruth: Tor Mark Press

Wood, Michael (1999) *In Search of England* London: Viking

Front cover: King Arthur window in Halls of Chivalry, Tintagel
Back cover: St Piran's Cross, Perranzabuloe
Frontispiece: Entrance to Trevorder House, former home of John Tregeagle